The Art of
Sales Management
75
Training Drills
To Build Confidence,
Excellence & Teamwork

Michael Delaware

If, And or But
Publishing Company

Published by

'If, And or But' Publishing Company
P.O. Box 2559
Battle Creek, Michigan 49016 USA
www.ifandorbutpublishing.com

ISBN-13: 978-0615908250 (If, And or But Publishing)
ISBN-10: 061590825X

For
Phil Voss &
Amanda Marie Skinner

Table of Contents

Introduction

    This book has been written to help sales managers and sales trainers to build confident sales people who function with teamwork. So often when someone mentions the concept of 'drills' they can easily conjure up images of late 19th century school houses with students sing-songing state capitals or other geographic locations they have learned.

    To others the concept of drills might be a marching band or a drill sergeant barking out orders to troops as they march along in unison. In truth drilling refers to practical exercises used to obtain application, retention and execution of certain skills or tools.

    This book is a resource of tools for sales managers to utilize to develop teamwork within a sales force, and also bring about excellence. It takes on the various aspects of sales disciplines from a variety of different drills to help develop skills.

In this book I will cover skills to improve understanding of the importance of communication, instill new thinking processes for deductive reasoning and bolster abilities to describe the products and services one is selling.

I will cover drills for speed and coordination, as well as drills for role playing and special drills for the showroom sales person. We will discuss one on one drilling and also collaborative problem solving drills. Finally we will cover a large selection of conference drills that can be used at larger sales conferences and meetings to help develop teamwork.

The benefits returned from training sales people through the use of drills are endless. Most notable as a result is teamwork resulting in higher productivity, increased sales and higher profits for any company.

So if you are a business owner who wants to see their sales increase, this is the book for you. If you are a sales manager who has been looking for ways to make your team more effective and climb to that next level, then this book will open many doors for you.

The concept of drilling for improved application has a long history with man. Armies have been using it for centuries to train their troops for battle. Professional sports teams dedicate several months before every regular season to drill their teams and prepare them for the regular season. Why should sales managers seeking to build an effective sales force be any different?

This book was written with compassion for the sale person who faces perhaps the most challenging job in any society. They sell the goods and services that keep any economy and currency moving. 'Currency' comes from the root word 'current' which refers to the energy of the flowing of a river.

Without the sales person out there selling, no economy, no currency or nation can long endure, much less prosper. So one can say this book is about achieving endless prosperity for the most valuable people who have their hands on the pump, pumping the blood of life through the very foundation of a society. They are the ones who keep the current of life energy moving in any civilization.

4 — The Art of Sales Management

Building Teamwork

The most important role for a sales manager is that of building teamwork among the sales people on his team. If one does not have teamwork, then one likely has no team. A group is essentially individuals, which may or may not be working together. Teamwork is cohesion and coordinated action to bring about maximized results.

There are many definitions of teamwork out there. Perhaps the best description as it relates to a sales team is: '*A cooperative effort on the part of a group of persons acting together as a coordinated unit towards the same interests, or a common cause or goal.*' Some of the essential ingredients to this definition are: '*same interests*' and '*common cause or goal*'.

When a group does not see they have the same interests, they cannot work together. If they are not working in the same direction, they are ultimately working in uncoordinated directions. With this in play, no one will arrive at the same place, and all will fall short of any stellar success. Achieving the summit of higher goals are only obtained through a group or team players focused and honed on the same goal and working together.

The foundation that a sales manager must build up from in order to create a 'team' starts with working with the individuals. To really build a team, there is a process one needs to follow in order to get everyone heading in the same direction. It follows this basic pattern:

1) Meet with every member of the team individually and privately. Have them read some basic definitions on words like 'goals', 'team', 'objectives' and 'coordination'. Find out what their individual interests are for being a part of the sales team. Try to get them to engage in a free discussion about their personal goals as a sales person, and what level they would like to achieve, etc. More importantly, however, talk to them about the value of helping others and get them to see that if they help others, others will help them, etc.

2) Once completed with the first step, meet with the group as a whole. Hold a meeting. Go over the definitions of 'team',

'coordination', 'similar interests' and 'goals'. Go over as many definitions of words that you feel they need in this group meeting to bring them all together on clarity of these concepts.

3) Once you have done the above, you are ready to take the next step which is drilling to create teamwork. They are called 'training drills' and these drills are done with individuals, segments of the team and the entire team together. They are the way you as a sales manager can mold the clay of a real team.

The first two steps are to establish agreement. The third step of drilling is to bring about a common understanding and trust. Training drills can be utilized one on one, at regular sales meetings, special weekend training sessions and even sales conferences. This book will cover training drills that can be done with small groups, and ones that can be done with a large conference consisting of hundreds of attendees.

All have the common purpose to bring about understanding and trust in different aspects of teamwork. The more a group of people can share drilling experiences as a team, the better they will be in the field of play in the business world. Much like a well trained and drilled basketball team that drives and passes the ball down the court trusting in their own team mates, and scoring basket after basket, a sales team too needs to build up similar teamwork.

It is not enough for one sales person to succeed in sales for the sales manager to be satisfied. True success is when all are brought up to the same level of success. Then one can really see the team as a whole reaching new unprecedented levels. The way to accomplish this is to get the members on your team to work together in a unified approach, passing the ball when needed with trust of the other sales people and knowing the ultimate goal is the closed sale, and the winning of the overall game.

The way one accomplishes this as a sales manager is through training drills to build team work. That is what will get them to break out of their individual shell of 'individualism' and become a true team. There is truth to the saying that there is no 'I' in *T-E-A-M'*. In order to have a group become a team, they need to see that they can understand and trust in their other players to follow established agreements with each other.

Established agreement on a 'code of conduct' is essential between team players. Codes allow all to feel in agreements. So rather than training on codes of conduct being done after group drilling, it makes sense that it would be included within the drills as well. This way one trains in an honest pattern of conduct within the team as one is honing their skills, and building their trust between each other. In fact there can be no trust without agreement on a code of conduct. So the chapter following this one will cover a basic code of conduct universal to sales people.

Building teamwork can be successfully accomplished with doing drills that require one to think through problems, look at problems from new angles as well as require the help of others to accomplish a goal.

There can be drills used to get the team players comfortable with each other, as well as into communication with each other as well. They can also require that they build something in collaboration, or solve larger problems with group insight.

The basic idea is to get them to stop looking at their success as strictly an individual goal, but to get them to expand into a frame of mind to become cognizant of group goals as being valuable too. In this way a sales manager can build a team who thinks of each other first, rather than themselves exclusively.

10 — The Art of Sales Management

A Basic Code of Conduct Between Sales People

Having an established code of conduct between sales people is an essential ingredient to maintaining a harmonious working environment. When no code is in place, there becomes a loose sense of what is acceptable and what is not, and injustices ultimately will occur. Therefore having a basic code of conduct for all sales people on your team to follow is something that should be in all of their initial training materials with your company.

Over the years, after having worked with many individual sales people and for many different sales organizations, I can safely say that the ones that have an agreed upon code among members are the ones who have the easiest time of it. It does not really matter how detailed the code is, as long as there is one. Having a code that covers the most common situations and occurrences makes it easier to sort things out when problems arise.

Here is a breakdown of a basic code of conduct for you to consider as a place to start:

1) Follow the *Golden Rule*: Do unto others as you would have them do unto to you.

2) A good honest transaction with a good satisfied customer is more valuable and important than your immediate compensation, so always give the greater importance to customer service.

3) Help other sales people, even if it means helping their client when they are not there.

4) Be willing to compromise when both sides are dealing honest with each other.

5) There are only two types of customers. Ones *you want to have* and ones *you want your competition to have.* Always be polite and friendly to both. Help the ones you want to have, and send the others on their way. It never makes sense to work with someone who you really do not want to work with. Nor does it make sense to pass on the troubled customer to a colleague in your same office.

6) Follow the rules of your company, and the laws concerning any product you are selling.

7) The person in front of you is more important than the person on the phone. The person who is on the phone is more important than the person you are writing an email or letter to. The customer contacting you either in person, on the phone or even in email or letter is more important than non-customers during business hours.

With some sharing of experiences with other sales people and your own customer service and business experiences, you can certainly expand or modify the above code. This is just here as a place to start for you to enlighten others on your team. Codes of conduct evolve with every organization and there will be unique details within each company you are a part of.

14 — The Art of Sales Management

The Skills of a Sales Person

If one goes searching through bookstores, there are numerous books available on closing techniques. Many surround the automotive industry, for example. There are experts who define every possible scenario a sales person can get into, and offers them solutions. A wise sales person is always seeking to learn new techniques and solutions for problems they encounter.

Training drills on these types of techniques typically rely on role playing. I have always preferred to think of it as a game of '*Let's Pretend*' as we so often found time for as a child in one way or another. Role playing is essentially a directed form of *pretending*, in which one walks through a scenario and experiments with probable solutions and outcomes.

This activity as a tool helps to build confidence and certainty when the sales person later faces a client and the situation becomes something similar to a *'Let's Pretend'* scenario he or she did with another sales person or the sales manager. They are more confident because they have been there before, even if the incident before was somewhat imaginary.

Repetition builds confidence and certainty. The skills of a sales person are best enhanced through the practice of drilling. Drilling allows one to practice refined techniques, and take them through a 'test run' of sorts. It also helps one develop and sharpen skills that one otherwise did not have. It can also open doors through means of a learning experience found nowhere else.

Some of the skills of a sales person can be learned from the writings of others conveyed in books. Others can be learned through seminars and lectures. Where is all comes together in practical application however is through the activity of drilling.

Why Drills & Not Just Study?

Why should drills be used in training sales people instead of strictly just giving them material to study or have them listen to lectures from experienced trainers? It is perhaps feasible that some sales managers would prefer to just hand out study materials such as the latest articles from 'Inc. Magazine' or provide a library of books for sales people to take advantage of and leave it at that.

The use of study materials has its place in the training process for sure, but it does not represent the entirely of the educational experience. Drilling puts the sales person into a scenario where they have to apply what they learn, and practice it. It bridges the gap between theoretical study and application.

Drilling provides a stop gap, if you will, between the sales person reading *about* techniques, and *applying them directly* with a customer. If you do not drill, then your sales people are reading the theory you offer and they are experimenting with this material on the customer. If their level of boldness is weak, then their experimental experience with the customer is weak, and they could be costing the company sales, customers and thus income.

Drilling becomes that step in between. It allows a sales person to reach down deep and apply material, and test it in a safe *'Let's Pretend'* environment without the direct risk of losing a customer if they err.

Drilling provides them a means to practice techniques, brain storm new ideas against other sales people, learn tried and true methods intimate to your products from experienced people, and make mistakes without liability. It thus becomes the perfect step between simply learning about it and actually using it on a prospect.

When one eventually applies what they learned on a live prospect, they have some experience with executing it, and can therefore proceed confidently. It certainly reduces the probability of errors being made in executing sales techniques on new customers. If someone leaves a drilling session after having practiced to a level of confidence with the techniques, then they are more likely to apply the material with the customers to a successful result.

Drills can also open doors for learning, and looking at aspects of things differently. They can raise awareness and shed light on weaknesses, providing opportunity for improvement.

Essentially if you are a sales manager, the use of drills is your best friend. It provides a means to iron out rough spots in any sales person; new or seasoned alike. The use of drills also helps to raise the bar of success even higher by increasing skills and knowledge.

20 — The Art of Sales Management

The Ideal Team

The ideal team for any sales manager is one that would be both competitive and cooperative among its players as they strive towards a common goal. Teams are built from new and seasoned sales people alike. New people especially are important as they bring in a fresh energy and often new contemporary ideas which can result in building a consistently modern team.

Quite often new salespeople are disregarded with a shrug of the shoulders and a thought of '*Let's see if they make it*' from experienced sales people. It is your responsibility as a sales manager to make sure that they do make it. Every person in sales can perhaps recall an experience where they walk into a new office one day and are asked by a salesperson *'Can I help you?'* as if they were a customer. Then the awkward and sometimes embarrassing need to respond with: *"No. I work here. I am a new salesperson. My name is…"*

Every sales manager should make it his or her duty to see to it that new salespeople are introduced to the other members of the team as an early action so as not to create this situation. Not only is this common courtesy, it is important to make them feel comfortable in the new environment and surroundings. Starting any job always comes with unfamiliarity of surroundings and people in the company. Help them by giving them the opportunity to become acquainted with everyone else on the team before a sales meeting, and then reintroduce them to the group at the first available meeting as well.

Building an ideal team requires as a basic step that everyone know each other. Learning to work together as a team is accomplished through team training. The best way to do this is to have the team of sales people work together in common drills so that they not only learn to rely on each other; they also understand other important points of teamwork. Drills help to accomplish the following in team building through the three 'C's' of teamwork: *Cooperation*, *Coordination* and *Consistency*.

Cooperation: Cooperation is necessary to have a team function together. It builds an operating basis where team members cooperate with each other and help each other on deals they are working together. Example: Salesperson 'A' has a client that drops in unannounced into the showroom or office, and needs help. An environment of 'cooperation' means that Salesperson 'B' will help this person in any way possible if Salesperson A is not there when this happens. Why? Because an environment of 'Cooperation' means players on a team help each other regardless if there is anything directly beneficial to them for doing so, and most importantly they help the customer. This is the right viewpoint.

Coordination: Coordination means to have team members working together to get things sold as a group. It involves a degree of Cooperation, but is also means following the agreements of the group. It means respecting another salesperson's customer and also their time off from work. It means adhering to the agreed upon schedule of the organization, as well as backing each other up when help is needed in a sale. No one likes to get that call on their day off from a boss asking them to come in to cover for someone who did not show for work. Certainly there are circumstances when this can happen that are justified, but coordination involves planning in advance whenever possible.

Consistency: Consistency is everyone being on the same page, do the same things and following the agreed upon rules and procedures day in and day out. It means creating an environment founded on predictability as opposed to one of unpredictability.

Knowing with certainty what one can expect from a fellow teammate and the team as a whole is created through consistency.

Another way to look at this is to also develop an attitude which I call the '**S.T.A.R.**' attitude, which comes from the first letters of '*Support*', '*Trust*', '*Alignment*' and '*Responsibility*'.

Support: Supporting each other even in difficult times and challenges. It involves knowing that one has the support of others when they need it as well. Being willing to support another sales person with help even when it is not asked for can also fall into this category.

Trust: Being worthy of trust is an important thing within a group of salespeople. When any member of the team is untrustworthy or dishonest, it begins the slow breakdown of team building. Working within an environment where people can be trusted unquestionably is important to teamwork. Codes of conduct that everyone agrees to can be essential to creating this atmosphere.

Alignment: Having all team members headed in the same direction towards a common goal is what 'alignment' is all about. When a team of sales people are all focused on the same goal or outcome, great things can happen. The group esprit' becomes contagious and the team working together can accomplish wonderful new achievements previously undreamed.

Responsibility: Responsibility encompasses all of the above: *Support, Trust* and *Alignment.* It includes being responsible on a personal level as a team member to do the necessary actions needed for success, as well as taking responsibility to see to it that the other members of your team do so as well. When one can be responsible for not only all of their own actions and outcomes, but take responsibility for all the others around one, a person begins to reach that unique level of greatness.

Sales team drills are designed to help accomplish each of the above points in a group of salespeople. Getting them to come together in a cohesive effort accounting for each of the above points is the very ingredients of building a successful team. The drills in this book are designed to help accomplish these essential ingredients, and make the members of your sales team see them as important too. Drills are a stepping stone to hammering a point home, and achieving understanding and agreement.

To create an ideal team, one uses drills to raise awareness and confidence, as well as create cohesion of teamwork. The test of a good drill would be whether it accomplishes directly or indirectly any of the above key points. Follow the three 'C's and the four points of 'STAR' and you will have the foundation for which success can be built.

26 — The Art of Sales Management

Communication Drills

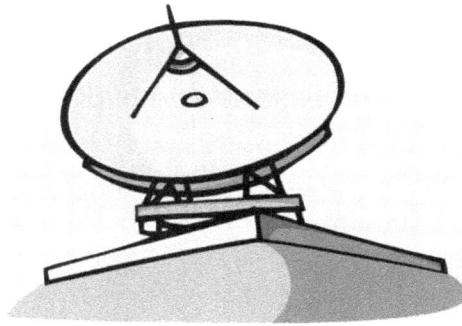

Communication drills are used to bring teams together and also can be a test on their ability to follow instructions. There can be many types of communication drills. Some work on an individual level, improving ones skills. Others work with groups to improve their ability to function together as a unit. In this section, we will be looking at drills that can be applied to bring a team together and have them begin working as a cohesive unit.

Some of these drills are quite challenging, and most can be run repeatedly at different times, and provide different results each time. The benefit of this is that a group will learn new things about themselves in using these drills, on every occasion of their use.

The drills in this section focus on skills to

improve and create clarity of instructions from the person delivering them, as well as the ability of the recipient to duplicate the instructions and apply them exactly. Those participating in these drills will learn to not only assume the viewpoint of the recipient when they deliver a message, but will also be willing to assume the viewpoint of the messenger when receiving one.

There are many lessons one learns as they improve communication skills. They learn to listen carefully, and really understand what is being said. They learn to deliver messages with clarity so that is can be understood.

They also learn the overall importance of good communication, and these drills help to demonstrate the outcome of poor communication being applied. When a sales person can grasp the importance of communication, they will continue to seek new knowledge on how to improve communication skills.

Good solid communication skills are the backbone of success for sales people, and quite often people do not realize that their own communication skills are lacking. The sales person will blame a poor outcome of a sales attempt on the customer, or some other environmental cause. The true reality is that all success in sales relies on good communication skills. These drills help to shed light on the importance of having these skills, and developing and improving them.

Communication Drill #1
Deliver the Message

One of the oldest communication drills to demonstrate the importance of message clarity and delivery is called *'Deliver the message'.* This is a drill designed to challenge duplication of communication through a group of people. It is a new and different level of challenge, as it deals with simply spoken communication. One can do this with one group of people, preferably sitting in a semi-circle either on the floor or at a large conference table.

Everyone sits shoulder to shoulder. A manager writes down a simple one sentence message on a piece of paper such as "The woods are dark at night" or "The moon is made of egg salad pasta". Something uncommonly said in everyday speech, and a little humor mixed in helps. He or she shows the piece of paper to the first person in the semi-circle and asks them to read it silently to themselves, and memorize it without letting it be seen by anyone else in the group. They are then instructed to whisper the message into the ear of the person next to them, but only one time.

The person who receives the message must then repeat it to the person next to them, and so forth down the line until it arrives at the last person on the other side of the semi-circle. Then this final person in the line must write down on a piece of paper what the message is and hand it to the manager who started the drill. The discipline in this drill is the teach the delivery of clearly understood communication as a point of coordination, but it also teaches the group the lesson of how communication can get distorted and altered as it passes from person to person.

For sales people to understand this is very important. Quite often one can be deceived by the belief that they can pitch their product to one spouse, and have that spouse go home and repeat the pitch to the other one successfully without the sales person being there, and have the sale occur. One learns from this drill that the likeliness of a customer delivering an exact copy of one's presentation and it being successful is highly unlikely. This drill also teaches the discipline of making sure sales people understand each other as a team, especially when communicating between each other as a group.

Quite often the first few times, especially with large groups, the message is extremely altered when it arrives at the end. I have found the odds are about 1 out of 10 times of it being successful on the first time through. This one is a lot of fun and stresses the valuable lessons on many levels: *Teamwork, basics of communication, clarity of the message one delivers, accuracy of message delivery, understanding each other, etc.*

Communication Drill #2
The Diagram Drill

There is a drill that can also work well to increase communication skills. It is called the 'diagram' drill. It challenges the participants to deliver effective instructions to each other blindly, just as if they were not in the same room but having a discussion over the phone or through email, etc.

The way this works is simple. Give each salesperson three sheets of paper, and pair them up in teams of two. Have the pairs sit on the floor with their backs to each other. They should find a place with ample room so other teams won't interfere. The teams will work independently of each other and are to remain in this position throughout the process, each unable to see what the other is doing. Instruct partner A of each team to draw three simple line diagrams, one on each piece of paper. Do not tell them what to draw, just something simple.

The drawings should all be different. Give them about three minutes for this activity. Make sure they do not show their drawings to their other team member.

In the first stage, partner B tries to correctly draw the same diagram by receiving instructions from partner A without being able to ask questions. Only partner A can speak. Partner B cannot speak or ask any questions. Allow five minutes for this stage.

In the second stage, partner B attempts to duplicate the second drawing, but this time is able to ask yes-or-no questions only. Again allow five minutes for this stage.

In the third stage, the task is repeated with the final drawing, and the partners are able to talk freely. Allow five minutes again for this stage.

After all three stages, allow the partners to look together at each other's drawings. Bring the group together in a large group for a discussion on communication and what they learned.

One should at the end of the drill have each team show before the entire group their three different results for each drawing in part A, B & C. The results will be astounding and perhaps bring about interesting realizations from the participants.

The stress of this drill is to get the team members to see the importance of listening to instructions, asking the right questions and being able to communicate precise instructions so as to arrive at a correct final product. This is perhaps one of the most challenging and thought provoking drills to help a team understand the value of precise communication.

Communication Drill #3
The Snowflake Game

The snowflake game is a classic communication drill for sales people. As a sales manager, one stands in front of the group of sales people and reads off a multiple step by step set of instructions on how to make a paper snow flake. No visual demonstration is given, just verbal instructions.

Then each member of the team is given a piece of paper and scissors and asked to make the snowflake. If they followed the directions properly, they arrive at a snowflake that matches one made previously by the sales manager. If not, then it means that more training is needed on the subject of listening and duplicating instructions given to them.

Give one white sheet of 8 ½ X 11 letter sized paper to each salesperson. Explain that you want them to follow the directions you are about the give without asking questions of you or anyone else present. The object is to have them all work individually, listening to the instructions and completing them.

One simply reads through the step by step directions quickly, without clarifying exactly what you mean:

> **1)** Fold the paper in half and tear off a top corner.

2) *Fold it in half again and tear off the top corner.*

3) *Fold it in half again and tear off the left corner.*

4) *Rotate the paper to the right three times and tear off the bottom corner.*

5) *Fold it in half again and tear off the middle piece.*

Instruct the group to unfold their papers and compare their snowflakes with those around them. They will find that their snowflakes may or may not match other members who did the drill. The ones who are farthest off are the ones who need more work on listening and understanding instructions.

This invites open discussion the subject of the importance of listening clearly to instructions, and making sure one understands. It transforms itself to not only listening to you as a sales manager, or any other company supervisor, but more importantly the customers they work with. If you can get the sales staff to see that they can always improve upon and strengthen their ability to listen and understand their customers, the end result is what both they and the customer wants.

The goals of such a drill are to help them understand the different ways that messages can be misinterpreted, the importance of really listening and understanding a customer's needs and also to recognize one can always improve upon their communication techniques.

Communication Drill #4
Getting to Know You

Sometimes when one is managing a team of sales people, the company can be so large that they are scattered across various regional territories. When one has an opportunity to gather them all together, it is advantageous to get them to interact with each other and bring about familiarity. Even sales people who do not cross territorial paths with each other often in the same company can find it invaluable to know their colleagues in other territories as customers quite often move about. Knowing the other members of your team when spread out can build up a network of inter-company referrals where no customer is lost because they move out of one's territory, as there is always a colleague who can pick up servicing them for example.

A drill that works well to break the ice, and get each sales person to know each other is to use the drill called '*Getting to Know You*'. A version of this was once featured in INC magazine as a helpful tool to get teams to know each other. Sometimes this drill is also referred to as the '*Tell the Truth*' game. The way it works is that you group your sales people up into different groups at a meeting, and have each one of them write down two truths about themselves, and one lie. It works best to have them write these on small index cards, with one truth or lie on each card, and their name on the top of it. They then mix up the cards, and hand their three cards to one person in the group who goes through each card and read's it to the group.

"Joe writes that he attended Clemson College as was part of the Football team" and the group must discuss it and try to determine if it is a truth or a lie. The fun is in discussing what is written, and once the group discusses it they vote as a group whether they think it is a truth or lie. They then turn to Joe and find out, and in so doing learn more about their colleague.

This is a very simple and easy communication drill to do with a sales team, and it has been found to be a great ice breaker for getting people to come together at sales meetings. It has the magic of inviting people to discuss and learn about each other in a manner that might otherwise take years of casual conversation to know.

Communication Drill #5
Model Building

Teamwork, group dynamics, communication skills, and achieving a stated goal can be a challenge to obtain with a new group of sales people. There is a more involved drill that can be done to facilitate this and improve group communication skills.

It is called '*Model Building*'. While reinforcing the process of teamwork to reach a common goal, this exercise utilizes discussion of communication and teamwork to learn about the importance of each person's role.

Participants are divided into groups of three who work together in two phases. First, each team designs and creates a structure without knowing they are building it for another team to duplicate. In the second phase the teams attempt to duplicate the design of another team while each member plays an assigned role.

GOALS:

1) To learn to work as a team using specific resources and instructions.

2) To experience challenges that can arise even with an obvious group goal.

3) To strengthen communication and team-

work skills.

MATERIALS & BASIC SET-UP:

1) Identical bags of simple building materials such as ball-and-sticks, toothpicks and marshmallows, or Lego's. Assure that each has bag has the same number of each color and size. Each bag should contain 60-80 pieces. Prepare two bags per team.

2) For each team, a non-transparent box large enough to contain an individual structure.

3) Ample room for the teams to work remotely from one another.

PREPARATION:

Divide the group into an even number of teams. A team size of three works best, however teams of four can be used. Attempt to divide them such that pairs of teams are of equal size. (For example, have six teams of three and two teams of four.) Do not make teams smaller than three.

Arrange the room so that teams can work remotely from each other. Place a row of chairs (one for each team) at a front table that is large enough to hold all of the boxes.

BACKGROUND:

When teams begin this project they tend to build with creativity and not malice. They don't know another team will need to duplicate their structure, and so they focus on creating a unique and interesting structure. While they usually start with an attitude of competition, participants soon discover that their success won't be measured by beating the others but will depend on their work as a group to achieve a goal. The activity is most effective when allowing these discoveries to play out naturally.

ACTIVITY:

Give each team one bag of materials and one box. Instruct them to build any kind of structure they wish without modifying the pieces. *(For example, they cannot bend or break toothpicks.)* Encourage creativity. Give them five minutes to complete their structures. Remind them to keep their structures away from the view of the other teams.

After five minutes, have each team put their structure into their box. Instruct the teams to assign roles to their members as Explainer, Messenger, or Builder. If there are four members to a team, two can be Messengers. The teams must make these assignments before proceeding.

The Explainer from each team will carry their team's box to the front table and place it at one of the chairs. The Explainers are then to choose a different box to sit in front of.

You can choose how to accomplish this, however, they should not be able to choose based on the structure in the box. They may have to do this with their backs to the table if the boxes do not have covers. Banker boxes work quite well for this drill.

Give each Builder another bag of materials. The Builder's job is to build a new structure identical to the model their Explainer has selected. They will do this with the information that the Messenger brings to them. The Explainer must tell the Messenger what the design looks like, including the color of the pieces. These are the rules:

1) Only the Explainer can view the model; not the Messenger or the Builder.

2) Only the Builder can touch the new structure or the raw materials.

3) Only the Messenger can speak to the Explainer or the Builder.

4) The Builder can ask the Messenger questions but cannot speak to the Explainer.

5) Messengers can keep going back and forth as much as necessary.

If there are two Messengers on a team, they must take turns going to the Explainer, and one cannot go to the Explainer until the other has completed communication with the Builder (no overlap of Messenger activities).

The Messengers cannot speak to each other and once a Messenger has started communication with the Builder, the other can no longer communicate with the Builder until he/she visits the Explainer again.

As an alternative, if you have two Messengers on every team, they should trade places between the Explainer and Builder simultaneously. This way, each cannot benefit from hearing the conversations of the other.

For an additional challenge, set a rule that the Messenger can't see what the Builder is building until the end. If you apply this rule, the Messenger must provide information from the Explainer without being able to point to or correct the Builder.

If choosing to add this rule, state it before this step of the drill starts. After an opportunity for questions, give the teams ten minutes to complete this phase.

Once this is done, have all three members from each team to get together with both structures to see how well they completed the task. The comparison of the two outcomes will be quite revealing to all involved.

DISCUSSION:

While every team had the same goal, it's likely that each worked very differently together. Take 10-15 minutes to discuss how the teams worked together and what they experienced and learned about communication. Use questions such as:

- *After building your structures the first time, what was your personal reaction when you realized what you would be doing next?*

- *Describe what it was like to be the 'Explainer', the 'Messenger', or the Builder'. Which role do you think was the most challenging? Why?*

- *If this had been an exceptionally important task involving communication, about how well would you consider your team has done? What would need to change for your team to be more effective as communicators?*

- *Was there any time during this activity when you wanted to cheat, maybe by peeking at the model? Why did or didn't you do this? (Relate this to real-life situations where people are given clear instructions on what is or isn't acceptable in the process of completing a task.)*

- *In what ways does this activity relate to how rumors and gossip spread? Were there times when you found yourself doubting the information being communicated to you? If it were a rumor going around, how would you have responded?*

Ask the salespeople to observe and compare the specific roles they work within the company or in other groups to which they belong. Remind them to look at interconnectedness and communication among people in different roles and how groups have successfully established those roles.

Encourage them to examine and note the importance aspects they learned about accomplishing group goals, communicating, and working as a team while restricted to specific rules and roles. You will find the outcome and results of this action to be quite enlightening for all involved.

46 — The Art of Sales Management

Descriptive Enhancement Drills

Descriptive enhancement drills help to train a sales person to be able to endlessly describe and present a product or service to a prospective buyer. Many times a client just needs to be given a reason to buy, and when a sales person can expound upon the many features, benefits and virtues of the product or service, it makes it easier for them to justify the purchase for themselves. Acquiring the skill to confidently deliver endless descriptions is an art that can be developed with practical drilling.

The drills in this section help a sales manager to train sales people to develop the skill of being able to continually talk to a customer with seemingly endless information about a product, even if the sales people themselves are new and unfamiliar with the product being sold.

These drills develop skills to be able to describe something from multiple points of view and elaborate on *applications, benefits* and *functions* to keep the client interested.

One of the secrets of selling a product quite often is just having the ability and the skills to keep a customer engaged in conversation about the product. By so doing, the customer will grow increasingly interested in buying the product. In this way a sales person can escort a customer smoothly down the path to making a purchase.

Sales managers can train sales people on techniques, closing tools and many other ways to get a customer to buy. However, the basic foundation of success is simply to be able to keep the client interested in the product one is trying to sell to them.

The way one can do this is to practice and develop the skill of being able to endlessly describe the product to the customer and continually enlighten them. With these basic drills, a sales manager can get any new or inexperienced sales person to know the basic skill of keeping a client engaged in conversation.

When a new sales person makes a first attempt at selling a product, they can quite often take a much longer time to sell a product to a prospective customer. That is okay with most sales managers, because the length of time one takes is secondary in importance to the outcome of a good sale.

However, when one drills a sales team and gives them a chance to apply what they learned, and then re-drills them again, the improvement ultimately become a faster and faster sales process.

The basic tools to get any new or experienced sales person selling more efficiently is to begin with descriptive enhancement drilling. That is what this section is all about.

50 — The Art of Sales Management

Descriptive Enhancement Drill #1

"Describe a _____"

There is value to being able to describe an item one is selling in a variety of ways to build upon the interest of the client. A drill for building upon a sales person's ability to continually describe a product to a customer is called 'Describe a ____'. The way this works is to have a group of sales people sit in front of a white board with one person standing there with a marker and call out descriptions one could use to describe a product.

For example, if one is selling custom made front doors, one would have them call out 100 ways they could describe that door to a client. *"Smooth grain", "Solid Hardwood", "Hand Made", "Custom Designed", "Custom Finished", "Fine Grain", etc.* As each one is named out, it is written on the white board for all to see. The more descriptions that are added, the more the board fills up.

The interaction of a group doing this drill together helps to expand the descriptive ability of all the members of the team as they share ideas. It can become incredible when you have a team of sales people selling a product that have a seemingly never-ending ability to fire off descriptions to a customer about a particular product to keep building their interest.

One can also expand this description drill to work over certain aspects of the product line. Taking the same example of the custom door above, perhaps doing a specific '*100 ways to describe an installation of a door*' would be a challenging drill. On the other side of this drill, you would have a team of sales people that had no trouble supplying the customer with an endless stream of descriptions about the benefits of paying for a custom installation.

This drill can have a variety of applications, and the more one applies this one the larger the arsenal of descriptions every member of the team will have in memory. They will tend to use the ones they are most comfortable with; however, when one is doing a brain storming session like the above, it is hard not to expand one's own supply of descriptions to use in the future. It is an incredible creative process to use for a group.

Descriptive Enhancement Drill #2

Object Descriptions

The prior drill involves building a vocabulary of descriptions for a single product. There is another useful drill to apply to build the skill of instantly shooting off a description of a variety of products, which can enable a salesperson to switch from one product to another as the customer accepts or rejects various items one is trying to sell.

A very fun and entertaining drill to use is the object description drill. The way this works is that a sales manager collects a variety of divergently different objects and places them all out of sight in a box out of the view of the sales staff. The sales staff seated in a group, facing the sales manager.

In this drill, the sales manager has a stop watch and sets it for one minute for each item they pull from the box. The sales manager reaches into the box, and holds up each item and the sales team begins calling out descriptions of the item on how they would describe it if selling it to a customer.

As each clock minute passes a new object it pulled from the box and the process is repeated. There should be at least 10-15 items in the box to run the drill. One could of course do it with more objects and make it longer if more time is allotted.

Some of the suggested items one could select are:

- *A towel*

- *A Teddy Bear*

- *A wrist watch*

- *An orange*

- *A Yo-yo*

- *A note pad*

- *A rubber band*

- *A roll of duct tape*

- *A paint brush*

- *A spoon*

- *A sea shell*

- *A bottle of perfume*

One can use one's imagination and even select items similar to what one is selling, such as a toy car for auto sales people, or a toy boat for recreational marine products, etc.

What one is trying to accomplish with this drill is the ability for the sales team to not only be able to describe items, but also be able to be creative and describe even new items to customers as they are added to inventory. One should include some easy objects, as well as some challenging ones to make it interesting.

Descriptive Enhancement Drill #3
Features & Benefits

Similar to the product description drills, one should use a similar drill for features and benefits. A product feature is described as 'A distinctive attribute or aspect of something'. A 'benefit' is described as: 'An advantage or profit gained from something'. So one is a detail about the item being sold, and the other is the outcome one can expect from owning such a product.

Sales people need to be able to discuss both features and benefits of a product to a customer. This is distinctly different from merely describing the product to the customer.

The way to do this drill is similar to the set up with the box and the variety of miscellaneous items in a box. The sales manager stands in front of the group of sales people who are seated, and pulls out each item one at a time for 1 minute durations on a stop watch.

The difference in this drill is that with each item one pulls out, the sales manager is asking them to call out as a group a 'feature' and then alternately a 'benefit'.

For example if one holds up a wrist watch, a feature might be *classic design* and a benefit might *know your time is accurate*.

When holding up a Teddy Bear a feature might be

'*fuzzy*' or '*hand-made*', whereas a benefit might be '*companionship for your kids*' or '*admiration from other bear collectors*' or something similar.

The concept of this drill is to get sales people thinking in terms in the differences between features and benefits, but also add to their arsenal in their sales presentations to the customers. Every sales person should understand the 'feature and benefit' part of a sales presentation.

It is also important to provide the customer with a benefit for each feature of the product or service. For example if the fabric for the couch one is selling comes in 18 different colors (*feature*) then one can easily find one that matches their existing decorating (*benefit*).

This drill can also be run as a silent drill where each sales person is given a note pad, and the sales manager holds up the item and they are given 60 seconds to write down as many features and benefits of the item in that given time frame.

One would then move on to the next items, and when they were all done, compare notes on each item as a group and share ideas. The more this drill is done as a group and as individuals, the better everyone on the sales team will become in their presentations.

Descriptive Enhancement Drill #4
Tie Downs

When one considers a 'tie down' in life, one perhaps thinks of those straps holding luggage on the top of a car or perhaps a rope keeping a tent secured to the ground in a wind storm.

In sales 'Tie Downs' are those things slipped in as points of agreement by a sales person in a presentation to a customer to create a continual simple affirmation that they are accepting the product or service.

An example of a 'Tie Down' statement might be *'Wouldn't you agree Mrs. Jones?'* or *'Isn't that so Mr. Rogers?'*

Getting the customer to affirm in acknowledgement that they agree at certain points of the presentation; *tying them down* ever so slowly, step by step, towards a final commitment.

A sales manager should have the sales team practice among themselves as a group in a sales meeting 'Tie Down' statements until they know them cold.

One way to do this is with the white board, having the team seated in front of it, calling out 'Tie Down' statements and writing them on the board one by one.

This can get their creativity flowing as a group, and it will become easier and easier.

A few more examples of 'Tie Down' statements are:

- *'Do you see how that can be?'*

- *'Don't you agree that color matches your décor?'*

- *'Isn't that a perfect match?'*

- *'See how that works?'*

- *'This is the right one, isn't it Mr. Jones?'*

Another way to drill this is to use flash cards with certain statements that are 'Tie Down' statements and ones that are not, and flash them to the group one by one asking if it is a usable one or not.

The idea behind this drill is to effectively train the sales people to build 'Tie Down' statements easily into their pitch throughout their sales presentation when working with customers, so that they build naturally and factually points of agreement throughout the process. In this way the customer will gradually become 'Tied Down' to a final commitment and ultimately make a sale.

Descriptive Enhancement Drill #5
Three Modes of Use

Another drill on the same theme of building the skills of a sales person through descriptions is the 'Three Modes of Use' Drill. The way this works is similar to the object description drill, but with the difference of when an item is held up for discussion, the sales people are asked to name off rapidly three modes of use that come to their mind when they see the object or picture.

What one is trying to do is get a creative flow of being able to describe application to a customer, even when it may not be the conventional ones. To make this challenging, require that each person in the group give three modes of use for the object that are different from the others, and have someone standing there writing them all down on a white board.

So one could hold up a photo of an automobile, and have someone say three easy and obvious ones such as 'transportation to work', 'transportation for the kids to school' or 'Travel' and think they are competed. However, if there are ten sales people in the room, there needs to be twenty-seven more descriptions created to move on to the next object or photo, so then it becomes a real challenge.

As they have to turn on their creative juices, they will begin to see other modes of use for the automobile and might come up with such unique ways to describe it as 'mobile surf board holder' and 'jet ski towing device', etc. The answers can be serious or humorous, it does not matter. What you will find when you use this drill the answers become colorful and interesting.

When customers experience these descriptions being applied on the floor from sales people talking to them about the cars (for example) they will know that your company is entirely different from the competitors selling similar cars.

The message will become more real and more intimate in detail too, and they will likely see that there is more creativity with your companies approach than the others they have perhaps visited. It is the difference between being drab and boring in ones approach to presenting a product, and being creative and alive.

This drill and the other ones on descriptive selling and 'features' and 'benefits' inspires creative and imaginative selling approaches, and if done correctly it will have a positive impact on the customers, and they will come back and refer others.

Deductive Reasoning Drills

Acquiring the skill of being able to follow a trail of information to learn important details about a client is an essential skill for a sales person to acquire. Quite often a customer will not reveal information openly to a sales person, so developing skills to be able to socially uncover that information can be essential to bring about success.

Deductive reasoning drills help a sales person learn to ask questions and uncover information to lay the foundation of a successful sales presentation. It helps them uncover a client's true motives for looking into the product they are selling, their resources and a great deal of other information that is valuable to know.

Learning the art of asking the right question or series of questions to get the client to open up to the sales person is a skill that comes with practice. The drills in this section offers a method in which a sales person can take on the challenge of uncovering information which can become a practical application to apply with customers.

Deductive Reasoning Drill #1
I've Got a Secret

'*I've Got a Secret*' was the name of a popular television show originally launched in 1952 featuring Gary Moore, which ran for twelve years. It also received a revival in 1964 with popular television show host Steve Allen. The show makes for a background model of a great training exercise for sales people.

Every potential customer has something they do not wish to reveal openly to a sales person, yet many times in order to be successful a sales person must find this secret in order to make a sale. Using deductive reasoning and developing a skill to ask precise questions to reveal the hidden secret is what this drill focuses upon. Knowing such a secret is often critical knowledge for the sales person which will enable a potential customer to make that purchase.

The way this drill works is the sales manager or trainer sits before the sales staff as a group, and openly states that they have a 'secret'. The staff with simple conversational questions only must attempt to deduce the secret.

With some practice it becomes a simple task of knowing which direction to take the line of questioning to reveal what is hidden. The sales manager should call out and give a buzzer sound to any questions that are not conversational, or improper to ask a customer in a real time situation. The training stress is to develop the skill for the sales team to be able to use conversations with a prospect to guide them to the secret.

Some secrets that the sales manager might start with could be along the following lines:

- *'I just inherited 1 million dollars from a deceased Uncle'*

- *'I have an insurance settlement that requires me to make a purchase of a new car by Friday'*

- *'I have a new baby on the way'*

- *'I am soon to be promoted at work'*

- *'My company is expanding to larger quarters next month, and need _____'*

- *'I am a medical doctor'*

- *'I am a close relative of a famous person'*

The above are just a few examples. The sales manager or trainer should use their imagination, and creativity to choose secrets that may be real for the sales people to encounter on a regular basis in the field or in the showroom when working with prospective customers.

The chosen secret should also have some sort of advantage to the sales person's presentation if revealed. Be sure to simulate a 'secret' which a customer might choose to hide from a sales person for fear of it being used to the sales person's advantage. In this way, the drill can become not only very real, but challenging.

This can be a fun, and entertaining drill for a sales meeting. It is a good practical exercise to develop the skills of being able to ask the right questions and uncover information about a prospective buyer without losing the prospect.

So as an additional training stress, the sales manager might also occasionally respond with 'I am offended that you should ask such a thing' or something similar to simulate a customer who has perhaps been pushed too far with a line of questions, or when a sales person becomes too openly invasive without being tactful.

Remember that this is a precise skill one is trying to develop, and the sharper one can train them to be smooth and friendly about their lines of questioning, the more effective they will be in using it with prospective buyers.

Deductive Reasoning Drill #2
What's in my Pocket?

In the famous novel the 'Hobbit' by JRR Tolkien, there is a scene where the character Bilbo is engaged in a game of riddles with a deceptive character names 'Gollum' who secretly intends to kill him in a dark cavern.

This same scene was recently included in the major motion picture of the same name released in 2013. In this game of riddles, Bilbo poses the question *'What is in my pocket?'* as his final riddle, because he has run out of conventional riddles that he can remember. Gollum has the ability to ask three questions to get clues as to the answer, and fails.

The game of *'What have I got in my pocket'* is also a good practical exercise for sales people to develop skills on finding out information about a prospective buyer in front of them. One can learn to ask questions about the customer to gather information about them to improve one's chances of making a sale.

The way to use this drill is to have the sales manager have an object in their pocket, and sit before the group of sales people and ask 'What have I got in my pocket'.

To begin they are given a total of 10 questions they may construct and ask to find out what the object is. They may ask only yes' and 'no' questions about its size, shape, texture, temperature, use, etc. They can ask anything about it, but they can only be questions that the sales manager can answer with a 'yes', 'no' or 'maybe'.

A suggested list of objects might be:

- *A food item, such as a radish or a grape*

- *A photo of a person or object*

- *A business card*

- *A small statue*

- *A stone*

- *A handkerchief*

- *A marble*

- *A piece of jewelry*

- *Tickets to an event*

- *A pocket knife*

One can get as creative as one wants with objects. It is suggested that one have a bag of items that have several objects, to make it easier to switch objects and continue the drill as needed. Use your creativity to have a variety of common and obscure objects to make it challenging.

If they fail to name the object after 10 questions, the drill is repeated with new object. Once they can get the answer in 10 questions, lower the number of questions to 5. To make it even more challenging lower it to a total of 3 questions. The skill one is trying to develop is their ability to be innately curious about a customer, and various aspects of their life. Similar to the '*I've got a secret drill*' this drill takes on a different line of questioning to find out precise details with the most limited amount of questions possible.

As a practical exercise, this drill is fun and you will be surprised on how it helps to develop the skill of deductive reasoning.

Deductive Reasoning Drill #3
Ten Questions to Three

There is a practical exercise to challenge sales people in a sales meeting that develops the skill of creating the perfect and precise questions they can use with meeting with customers.

The way this works is to have the sales staff sitting in a group facing the sales manager or trainer with a white board and marker. The sales manager asks the group to come up with 10 questions that they consider to be the best ones to ask a customer in order to get the precise information they need to make a sale. Have them work together, as a group, to refine the wording of the questions, and narrow down the selection to the 10 best ones they all agree on.

Each question is written on the board in front of them, and edits are made as they revise them. Once they are satisfied as a group that these are the 10 best questions to ask, then tell them that they now must erase seven of the questions and isolate the three best questions in the entire list.

Tell them that in the scenario of a common meeting with a customer, they may only have the limited opportunity to ask a maximum number of three questions of a customer. Ask them to isolate the three best from that list.

You will find in doing this drill that several things

can happen:

    A. *They realize some of the questions could be consolidated*

    B. *Some questions will be more important to know the answers to for certain sales people, and others will determine that other questions are more important to them.*

    C. *They may even refine or re-word their previous questions yet again.*

    D. *They will realize some questions need to be more precise.*

    E. *They will also come to realize that some questions need to be broader.*

Whenever a group is given the flexibility to select from a large number like ten, there is a tendency to be loose with criteria to arrive at the outcome. When the selection is narrowed to three, they will refine their line of questioning to a more precise list of information they feel is most important to know.

There is no right and wrong to this drill, and there are no right and wrong questions. What one is attempting to do is to get them to see that they can be more exact and precise in their questions, and when they develop them they should memorize and use them over and over. However, at the same time they should be flexible to adjust them as circumstances change.

To expand this drill further, one should begin with a customer profile. Tell them the prospective buyer is a young woman who has walked into the showroom with a brochure from a competitor, and ask them to come up with 10 questions. Then repeat the above drill and ask them to refine it down to three. Once that is done, switch the profile of the customer to say an *elderly man with a cane* accompanied by *a small child* and so on.

Ask them to look at their selected three questions, and see if they would be the precise ones to ask this prospect. The discussion on this can become an intriguing one. However, it will give them insight into the differences between precise, general and adaptable questions for their arsenal in their sales presentation.

They will also gain an advantage of listening to the insight of each other's viewpoints and the different approaches that might be taken. Utilizing this drill frequently can help to develop good communication skills and the ability to adapt questions, and at the same time make them precise enough to gain the information needed to make a sale.

Deductive Reasoning Drill #4
What's My Job?

A similar style of deductive reasoning drills is one called *'What is my job?'* It follows a similar set up with the sales staff seated in front of a sales manager, and this time they all have note pads with them and a pen.

The sales manager chooses a profession that is common and the name of a local company and does not disclose this to the sales staff. He or she write this on a piece of paper or note card and lays it facing down on a table in front of the group.

The sales people in the group are given a total of 10 questions they may ask the sales manager about what his job is. The only two questions they may not ask are: 'Where do you work?' and 'What is your job?'

The challenge is for sales people to determine what people do for a living through casual conversation without asking them directly. Another training stress is that each salesperson in the group may only ask one question. If there are more than ten in the group, they are to decide which of the ten will ask a question. If there are less than ten, then some may be allowed to ask two.

The remaining group members may engage in a discussion to develop questions, but it is up to the individuals to decide what will be the important question to ask next. The sales manager when asked the questions must never answer directly what the job is, and be evasive about the name of the company. However, they must answer all other direct questions.

This is an interesting practical exercise in deduction and helps to develop skills on finding out indirectly information about a customer, without asking them directly. No one may guess the job aloud. They are to remain silent about their conclusions.

When all 10 questions are asked, it is for the sales people individually to write down on their note pads what they think the person's job is and where they work after the ten questions are asked. The sheets are handed up the sales manager, and read one by one to the group.

Finally the card with the true job is revealed, and they can all find out how well they did and who, if any, selected the correct job and place of business.

When they have guessed the first job and place of business, the sales manager should choose a more challenging one with a less common profession and business. It is best to use real jobs and names of businesses that exist, and it should be somehow located or within the territory of the sales people to make it more realistic. This can be an very challenging game, and it helps to develop good detective skills with your sales staff.

Deductive Reasoning Drill #5
The Magic Box

There is a very old practical exercise to help expand ones frame of mind in terms of thinking through problems. It has been called by many names, and perhaps is best described as the 'The Magic Box' drill. It is more of a visual puzzle for one to look at, and come up with a solution. Look at the following image.

The test of this exercise is to draw three lines consecutively without lifting the pencil off the paper. The three lines drawn must intersect all nine dots on the page. Take some time to examine this and try to solve it.

If you cannot, move on to the next page for the solution.

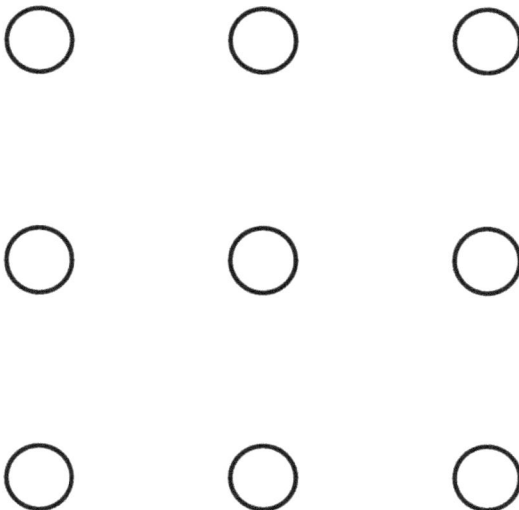

O   O   O

O   O   O

O   O   O

When you now look at the solution, it is easy to see that one's frame of mind in thinking with the solution tends to limit one to thinking *inside the box.* To solve the problem, one needs to think *outside the box.* The lesson here at its most fundamental is that one has a need to be able to be original and sometimes unconventional in one's thinking to resolve problems.

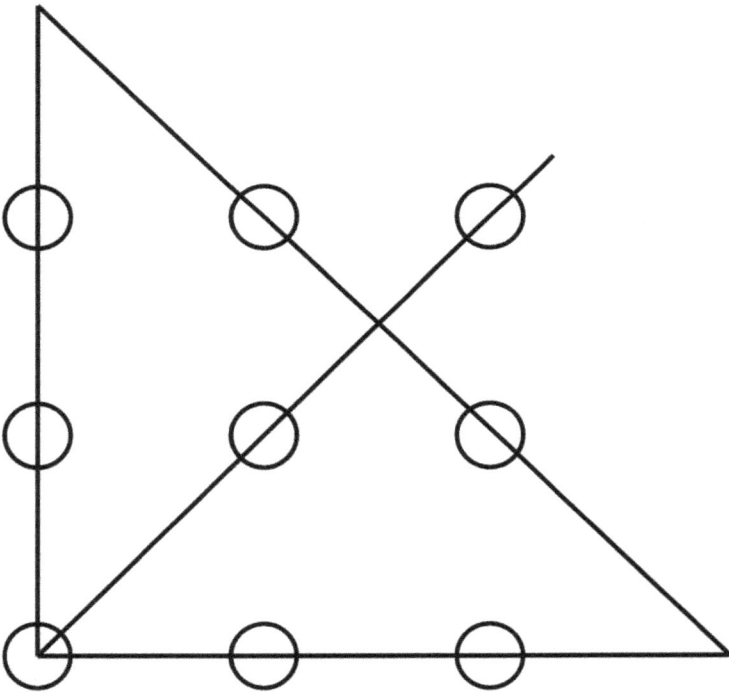

Such an understanding of this drill can be quite valuable to a salesperson. When they can confront problems in terms of 'thinking outside the box' they can resolve other issues that may come up with dealing with one on one presentation with a prospective buyer. Sometimes a salesperson is required to be creative in their thinking in order to help a customer arrive at a purchase.

Of course when someone is already familiar with this puzzle and drill, they should be asked to remain silent when it is being presented to others who have not seen it. The important task is the get them to experience the drill for the first time, and receive a raised awareness in creative thinking from the experience of discovering the solution for the first time.

Memorization Drills

In today's school systems it is quite often found to see classroom instruction drifting away from memorization of facts as an essential to education, and focusing more on functional application. This is largely due to facts and information being so readily available on the internet that it quite easily gets disregarded.

However, in the field of sales it is important to know facts and information in memory for many reasons. One can take added time out of a sales presentation by answering a client's question swiftly without having to refer to some other reference and it can also be useful for simply smoothing customer relations.

Being in a position to answer a direct question as to whether a model is available in a particular size, color or with certain features immediately when the client asks it allows a sales person to stay in control of a sales presentation.

The moment they have to stop and say *'Let me go find the answer to that question sir'* it not only adds additional time to the sales presentation, but is also lowers their credibility with the client and causes them to lose a degree of control.

Knowing prices, product descriptions, uses, locations and even area codes a client is calling from can be extremely useful for sales people to have working familiarity with. One can achieve this through the use of practical exercises.   One should be able to know the important features, characteristics, delivery and installation options, value packages, etc. cold on any product or service one is selling.

The following series of drills can be useful to apply as a practical exercise to increase an individual sales person's knowledge of your products and services, as well as build a foundation of confidence and certainty. One can also use these drills on a team of sales people at a meeting or conference.

Memorization Drill #1
Name Recognition

'*Name Recognition*' is another group drill that is a lot of fun. It works particularly well with teaching sales people the discipline of remembering names. This one works best with a group of 20-30 people minimum. The team is gathered together in a room, and each given a slip of paper which contains a name.

These names can be silly or common, or more difficult as one repeats the drill. They are to read and memorize the name given to them. Once everyone has looked at their name, then they are all asked to stand up and greet 5 to 10 people each in the room (the sales manager should choose a number for each time the drill is run, progressing in difficulty) and introduce themselves, and remember the other person's name.

Once everyone has done that, then they all sit back down and are either given a sheet of paper to write down the names of the people they just met, or better yet asked individually as they go around the room to and name correctly the names of the 5 -10 people they just met. This is a test of recall, and can be expanded in difficulty to include a name and an occupation on each slip of paper.

So it runs something like this: "*Hello, my name is Peter Rabbit and I am an Organic Vegetable Specialist*" followed by "*Pleased to meet you, my name is Solomon*

Grundy and I am a soap and laundry detergent analyst", etc.

This drill should progress in difficultly from silly, easy to remember names, to a mix of common names like 'Smith; and 'Jones' to more complex names one can pull from a common phone book.

What one is looking for as a developed discipline is for sales people to capture someone's name and occupation upon first greeting, and remember it so as to avoid asking the customer later *"What did you say your name was?"*

Whenever you can build a team that can learn this skill, the customer will feel more important and have more affinity for the sales person for them having remembered who they are and what they did. It is a great drill, and one that can be done at sales meetings as often as one wants to, and the difficulty can be increased as one chooses. One can also substitute customer names for product names and their parts to teach the names of these items to a new group of salespeople if one chooses.

The basic skill here is a test and challenge of recall, and the more one practices it, the better they can become at it. The challenge to remember customers names and people one works with can be a grueling task at time, and drills such as these help the sales person to develop memory keys for themselves on their own terms to make it easier and stress the importance to remember a person's name.

One of the training stresses on this drill can also be to have the sales person doing the drill discipline themselves to repeat the name they learn to themselves three times before responding or moving on to another question with the client, all the same time looking at the customer as a form of memory recognition practice.

Memorization Drill #2

Customer Recognition

When a sales person has been selling awhile, it is easy to forget names of people they have met. Working through a drill to help them with this problem can be a great help. The drill called 'customer recognition' has two fundamental steps: '*Memorization*' and '*Triggers*'.

This drill can first be done in front of a white board with drawings or photos attached to it. One puts up on the board faces of a dozen people, it does not matter who it is, they simply needs to be the faces of people the sales person does not know. Below each person write a name. Ask the sales person to look at the face, and then the name separately.

Then ask them to look at the picture again and find something unique about it that they can remember in the future. It could be the hair color of the person, the hair style, their lips, eyes, nose, ears, etc. Once they have done this, ask them to remember the name with that detail about the person. Explain to them that this detail will become their 'trigger' for remembering the person again in the future.

Once they have done this, erase the name, and ask them to look again at the face. Then take a 15 minute break, or move onto another subject for awhile. Come back to this drill after some time has elapsed and the sales person's attention has been placed on other things.

Scramble the pictures, and place them back on the board again. Ask the sales person to write down the name of the person under each photo. If they have been successful with following the instructions of the drill, they will be able to correctly name each of the people in the photos.

Once they have done this initial drill step correctly, ask them to apply this technique with the next 10 to 20 people they meet. Look at the person, and remember a personal detail about each, and assign the name of the person to that detail. With practice, this method of memorization of the person's name with the use of a trigger or detail of the person will help them to be more successful at this in the future.

Memorization Drill #3
Remember the Cost

I good drill to use at sales meetings is the *'remember the prices'* drill. It can also be called *'remember the cost'.* The drill consists of having the sales manager standing in front of a white board with a marker.

The drill can be done with either writing down the description of the product or item, or holding up a photo of the item. The items of course are the products and services the company sells. What the sales manager is trying to accomplish with this memorization drill is to get the group to remember the cost or price of the product or service on sight.

It works best with showing the item or description of it and asking what is the price of this item? What is it with a package discount? What is it with a delivery or installation?

Whatever the item or service is, the challenge here is the develop a certainty in the group on what the prices are without always having to have them consult a price tag, catalogue or sale manager. They can be in a better position to answer people's questions, and also build confidence on what types of packages they can offer someone.

This drill of course works well in training sales people on the value packages (if any) that the company offers, or quantity item sales, etc. Is everyone going to know the exact price all the time? This is probably unlikely if you have a lot of inventory and items, however, drilling can build in a level of certainty which will reduce having the sales person lose valuable time with the customer calculating numbers when they should be selling and getting the person committed to buying. Even if the sales people are trained to discuss price ranges instead of exact prices, this drill can be of infinite value.

Sometimes quoting a range with certain services or products is a safer way to go, especially when dealing with products that fluctuate in cost due to changes in the market place. Also things like delivery costs and installation costs can be difficult to price without firming up more exact details.

However, having sales people being comfortable with quoting prices is what the sales manager is looking for, and any drilling that one can do with them on this will enable them to be able to exude confidence when in front of the customers.

Memorization Drill #4
The Map Drill

Whenever a sales person is required to canvas an area to sell products, it is always valuable to drill familiarity with the locations they will be traveling to in their territory. This drill can be done with an individual or groups who are covering an area. One takes a map of the city, county or region that is being assigned. One gives each sales person some time to study the map individually.

Then once the individual study is done, pin the map up on a wall and with a pointer selects various areas on the map and says 'Where is this?' requiring the sales person to recite the name for the area. This can be done for neighborhoods, suburbs, boroughs, cities, counties, etc. The idea is that one becomes routinely familiar with the map of the area, which will make it easier to navigate.

Too many times today sales people become too dependent on electronic devices, and never really learn the area. It is important to not only know the names of the cities and counties, but one also must learn about the key landmarks in the communities.

One should also do this drill with locations of land marks such as ball stadiums, statues, museums, parks, etc. Anything that would be considered the communities highlight that might come up in a routine conversation with a client. Knowledge of an area where one is working on a regular basis is important to build up relationships and confidence with those that live and work there.

So taking some time to drill the maps of the area, and locations and even distances and roadways can be not only helpful but a fun way to draw a connection and create interest in the region they are assigned. If a sales person is interested in an area, they will be excited to work it.

Memorization Drill #5
Area Code Recognition

Whenever a sales person is required to work phone lines, and receive calls for services and products from all over the country, it can be quite useful for them to learn telephone area codes for faster recognition of where the client is located.

Certainly one can keep an area code list on their desk, and refer to this in conversation. However, what if one is not at a desk and the phone they are using does not identify the city or State they are calling from? Obviously this is a skill that one can drill with if they find it useful.

Sometimes when one is dealing with clients all over the country it is useful to know area code recognition on sight to gain instant familiarity. One can see the area code and know the person is calling from New York or Louisiana and take an entirely different approach to the call because one is instantly familiar with where they are calling from.

One of the best ways to drill this is to use flash cards and lists to refer to. One prints out a list of all the national area codes, and places a copy into the hands of each sales person in the group. Then one has some index cards draw up with several common area codes on them, and flashes them in front of the group.

Each time one holds up a card with an area code

on it and asks 'What State?' Every time they don't know, or guess wrong, have them refer to the list in their lap. Keep doing this on a regular basis for 10-15 minutes a day at the beginning of sales meetings, and soon they will begin to develop the skill to recognize them on sight.

This can be an interesting skill to develop and new and seasoned sales people alike can often see the practical application of such a drill when they are receiving calls from all over the country.

Memorization Drill #6

Kumon

'Kumon' is an extracurricular Japanese system of worksheet drills for students outside of mainstream school work. Basic Skills practice cards are designed and used in many different formats.

The approach uses a game board, and sometimes a lotto format or flashcards. It is typically a tutoring program approach for students which can work for a variety of subjects of study, but is often associated with the study of mathematics and reading. A similar program can be used to drill sales people on product knowledge, prices and other services the company offers.

The Kumon program is an individualized study approach and it allows a person to study at their own pace as they progress through check sheets and drill packs.

A similar program could be developed for your company where work sheets are compiled on product knowledge, price sheets and other services and trained in through practical memorization steps similar to this approach. That is why this program is suggested here. It helps to take a step by step approach to enable them to build a solid grasp on the material.

This can be a valuable way to approach the problem in companies with large amounts of products and services within a company catalogue. This kind of drilling and study could be implemented with a daily study regimen for a few hours.

Memorization Drill #7

Product Description

To know how to describe clearly and effectively the product one is selling is essential to a smooth and successful sales presentation. Taking time with sales people individually and as a group to drill the descriptions of the products can be essential.

One of the best sequences to follow in product description drills is to take a three step memorization approach:

1. *Verbal recognition*

2. *Flash card recognition*

3. *Image recognition*

Verbal recognition: This consists of simply having the sales manager hold up a catalog or product description sheet and read off item by item, and ask the sales person or group to repeat it back after each line.

Flash Card recognition: Once the product description sheet has been read through and repeated back a few times, then pull out the flash cards. The flash cards should consist of a written description each item individually, one per card. Hold each one up, and have the group call out what it is and recite the description.

Once they have done this for a few times, go

through the flash cards again and have them describe each item individually in their own words as the sales manager points them out one by one.

Image recognition: This step is similar to the flash cards, except these cards have no writing and only photos of the items. This is so the sales person and the group can gain the skill of knowing each items name from visual reference. This step can also be done with an exact description of the item and then the sales person's description in their own words.

What one is trying to accomplish with this drill is to have a team that knows the description of their products cold. One should be able to take an entire team through the essential products they are selling, and raise their certainty and confidence on being able to talk about each and every one of them. They should also be able to visually recognize the product and be able to point it out and describe it.

For larger catalogs in companies with vast quantities of products, this drill could be done is sections of the catalog or having the sales manager select only the most salient products from the entire lot that would be essential for them to know cold.

This same drill can be used for different aspects of a product line, such as the various colors and accessories related to the main product.

The training discipline would be to keep going through this drill on a regular basis to a point where the team of sales people can rapidly one after the other be able to recite and describe each product, feature or accessory one is selling. At the very least your team will have a greater working familiarity with the products they are selling.

Memorization Drill #8
Myanmar Rote

In a school absent of textbooks such as in schools in Burma (known locally as Myanmar) the practical way of delivering instruction is through rote learning practices.

This system involves an instructor standing in front of a chalkboard writing down words and phrases and then having the class repeat the words and phrases over and over again until they retain the information and can recite it verbatim.

This system of learning has not catapulted Burmese education into the stratosphere on a global scale; however, the method of rote learning can be valuable training of groups such a team of sales people. A sales manager can avail themselves of such a system of learning by utilizing this in sales meetings to get the group to know cold key product features, sales rules, sales procedures, etc.

There is no limit to the information that can be drilled in using this system as it is effective on a short term training basis.

The drill consists of simply using a white board or chalk board with key phrases or information written on them. The sales manager reads the phrase aloud, and asks the sales team to repeat it aloud back. This process is repeated back and forth until the group can chant it in uniform repetition and with confidence. This practical exercise may seem amusing or odd the first time one drills it, but after time one can see the results as the sales team comes to know and apply the material one is drilling them on regularly.

This drill for learning is based on an old system that pre-dates many modern systems of education. It may not be superior to textbook learning approach; it is nonetheless effective in getting a group to absorb information in spoon fed amounts. The only way to know if this will work for you is to try it.

Collaboration Drills

Collaboration drills consist of bringing a group of sales people together and having them work through problems and come up with shared solutions that they can all utilize in their own sales presentations. It is a moderated discussion with the sales manager and the sales team. It usually involves a white board where ideas are written down and discussed in detail. It is a perfect type of drill for any sales meeting.

In this chapter we are going to cover five very effective topics to address for any sales team in a collaborative drill session of this type. Whenever one engages these five topics with a group of sales people, one usually discovers that all the team become involved in the discussion, new and experienced alike. The reason for this is due to the fact these topics are ever expanding and ever changing scenarios that the sales person commonly faces. One can never have too many tools in their tool box to address these when working with customers.

Topic number 1: Common Objections

Every product being sold has an entire field of objections to buying that product that are originated by the prospective customer. *'Not my color', 'Not now', 'Price too high', 'I need to wait to buy until___',* etc. Objections, objections, objections... They are endless. Every prospective buyer will throw an objection at a sales person, and it is up the skill of the sales person to resolve the objection and move past it to continue down the road to the sale. Having a collaborative discussion among your sales staff on common objections faced and successful rebuttals used is an essential training tool.

This kind of forum can also serve as a medium to develop new ways to resolve an objection that has previous seemed irresolvable by an individual sales person. Sometimes new objections arise that no one in the group has experienced before, and together the team can come up with theoretical ways to attack these when they arise again until they develop one that is deadly and handles it every time.

Topic number 2: 'Best Price' Rebuttals

Sometimes a sales person encounters a particular client that is almost robotic in their repeated request for the 'best price'. Opening a group collaborative discussion on how to counter this kind of customer origination can be quite useful. Sometimes combating the 'best price' is to turn to the customer and deliver to them a raised price to stop them in their tracks. Other times it is to combat it with value added options, and in some cases, even though it is least desirable, is to lower the price at a discount. Such a discussion can yield many ways to resolve the 'best price' customer.

Topic number 3: '*Be Back*' resolvers

One of the most frustrating experiences for a sales person is to spend time with a client on the showroom floor, and get close to a sale, only to have the customer get up and leave saying they will 'be back'. Sometimes that client comes back, and other times they do not. Conducting a group collaborative discussion between sales people on this topic can also yield some interesting results.

How can one get the person to buy before they leave? What can be said to stop them in their tracks? If they must leave, what can be said or done to retain them or make sure they return? What magic can a sales person use to pursue the client later, get them back in or contact them by phone to close the sale? All of these points can yield excellent discussion, and the end results will only be a more effective sales team combating this particular problem.

Topic number 4: The changing objection customer

Addressing the type of customer who changes their objection every time one is resolved is easy. One just continues to resolve objection after objection until they run out and one closes the sale. However, sometimes sales people can get exhausted with this type of customer and give up. Other times they run out of ideas to resolve the numerous objections. Spending time discussing this type of customer as a group and coming up with collaborative solutions can yield some positive results. Each and every sales person participating in such a group discussion will gain new insight into objection resolution, and more tenacity to continue on with such a client if they understand what it happening.

Topic number 5: The legitimate objection customer

Sometimes a customer comes up with a legitimate objection to buying that does not seem to resolve with standard objection resolution. A customer throws out an objection that they have to *'wait because they do not have the money'* to purchase. No matter how the sales person tries to help the person resolve this legitimate objection, the customer continues to return to the same objection and is non-moving on it. In salesmanship, there is a basic law that one needs to learn. It goes like this: If a customer repeats the same objection over and over again, it is classified as a *'legitimate objection'*. The only way to resolve a 'legitimate objection' is to hit the customer with the same objection as the reason they need to buy the product or service.

This *'fighting fire with fire'* response is the only tool that defuses this type of objection. For example: A person says *'I cannot buy this _____ because I do not have any money'* as a legitimate objection. The sales person rather than try to solve to problem in any other way says back to the customer *'You need to buy this _____ because you do not have any money. Having this _____ will enable you to have money'* and pursues this line of response in varying ways over and over again as needed.

The sales person is combating the 'legitimate objection' with the same *'legitimate objection'* as the solution. Group discussion on this point can yield some interesting collaborative techniques to handle any legitimate objections with the same legitimate objections.

Call it 'water for water', 'fire for fire' or whatever you choose. After a team of sales people are drilled on this type of objection they can become irresistible to any customer. I have even heard sales people refer to this technique as the *'Jedi Mind Trick'* because it appears to work magically like that scene from the original Star Wars with Obi Wan Kenobi getting past the Storm Troopers at the checkpoint. If done correctly, it has a way of neutralizing the *legitimate objection* for good.

Role Playing Drills

One of the best ways to drill sales people is through the use of role playing. This type of drilling is done one on one with a sales manager, sales trainer or experienced sale person and the sales person (or 'trainee') doing the drill.

The trainer either sits across from the trainee in chairs facing each other, or seated across a table or standing up in a showroom sales environment. This type of drill can also be done over a telephone to train sales people on the phone.

The trainer assumes the role of a prospective customer, and the trainee assumes the role of a sales person trying to sell that person. This approach seeks to simulate a sales scenario for the trainee to work their way through, and develop practice with handling customers.

It is important for the trainer helping the trainee do the drill to have a working understanding of the situations the person being trained may face, and give them realistic situations to learn from.

The trainer also needs to understand that one does not take too steep an approach, so as to build the skills of the sales person with an increased step by step level of skill.

Some of the topics that can be role played to help a trainee though various scenarios should be:

- *Resolving customer objections*

- *Dealing with an angry customer*

- *Dealing with a scattered customer*

- *Dealing with a silent or non-communicative customer*

- *Dealing with a mysterious or shady customer*

- *Working with a person with a distracting child*

- *Dealing with a customer who won't stop talking*

- *Dealing with a scared customer*

- *Selling the product or service*

- *Selling value added packages to a sale*

- *Up-selling the customer to a more expensive model*

- *Smoothly passing off the customer to a more experienced sales person*

- *Dealing with an intimidating customer*

- *Dealing with a rude customer*

- *Dealing with a flirtatious customer*

- *Dealing with a sad or grief-stricken customer*

- *Getting the customer to agree to a purchase*

- *Transitioning from presentation to signing papers*

There can be many, many scenarios that a sales person can experience. Role playing can be used to train new people and experienced alike. It does not just have to be used when a sales person starts. This type of drilling should be used over and over again as a daily or weekly practice.

Sales people meet new people every day, and have new experiences all the time. Whenever they encounter a new situation, particularly one that they were not successful in making a sale with, the situation should be role played to help the sales person work through various ways they could address this in the future and remain in control. Using this type of drilling this way builds a team of sales people who learn from their experiences, and increase their skills.

A sales manager should be able to recognize when a sales person struggles with a particular type of client or sales situation, and help them work through it with role playing. Sometimes a new situation can also crop up which one sales person experiences and handles successfully, but because it is new, this scenario should be role played with other sales people on the team so they can learn from this experience as well.

Role playing drills are a very effective tool to help a sales person build up confidence, work through problems and develop new skills. This type of drilling should be used often when training sales people.

Real Time Drills

Real time drills are drills consist of taking the sales person and placing them in a semi-controlled situation dealing with real people. They can consist of drills that require them to practice their people skills on general public on the street to first sales presentations in front of real customers. They are very 'real' as they involve real people, and none of it is staged and the outcome is never predictable.

In this section I will be addressing two basic types of real time drills:

A. *Ones which are done with random people to give the sales person experience with talking to strangers.*

B. *Ones where they are working with real customers on their first presentations.*

Both kinds of drills involve having a sales manager or sales trainer present, coaching them through the experience or just shadowing them as they go through the drill and being there to help them out only if they get into trouble.

These are very good drills to help build up a person's confidence and it also allows the sales manager or trainer to see what the sales persons strengths are and what areas they need work on.

Real Time Drill #1
Pat, Slap, Pat...

There is a basic format for training a new sales person when they go on their first few presentations with a real customer that is customarily called '*Pat, Slap, Pat*'. It refers to the role that the sales manager or trainer holds when shadowing a new trainee on their first presentations. It is important to let them do the presentation, and only get involved when it is absolutely necessary.

The sales manager or trainer simply is present during the presentation, and remains silent throughout and only comes into the presentation if the sales person asks them to or they observe some gross glaring mistake that could cost the company money. Those are typically the two extreme situations: A '*cry for help*' or a '*cataclysmic event*' resulting in a lost customer, or an undersold product through a glaring mistake, or something similar.

When the presentation is completed, and the customer is gone or they leave the customers home, the sales manager or trainer sits down with the sales person and goes through the presentation and what happened.

They first find something good to say about how it went. This is the '*pat*' on the back. They then go over what is needed to correct, or the errors that were made and correct them. This is the '*slap*'. The sales manager then wraps up with finding something good to say about the sales person's presentation '*pat*' and leaves the training/correction session on a good note of encouragement.

It is important to remember when training a new person that one encourages and points out the good aspects of their presentation, before correcting them on what they did wrong. Then as stated above, one ends with again reminding them what they did right, so that they leave with a sense of accomplishment.

Real Time Drill #2
Silent Observation

An important step early on is to get sales people to *really look* at people. A way to do this is with an introductory drill to have them do what is best described as 'Silent Observation'.

The way this works is to have the sales manager take the sales trainee to a public location where there are a lot of people, such as a park or shopping mall. They sit down side by side and watch people walking by. The sales manager asks the sales person to note observations about people, by selecting people out of the crowd as they walk by. They silently observe the person, and the sales person is asked to describe their observations only without any bias.

Assumptions such as *'That person is poor'* or *'That person is a snob'* is tossed aside by the sales manager as being unproven. *"How do you know they are poor?"* the sales manager should challenge, and also *"How have you concluded they are a snob?"* The sales person should be grilled for anything assumption that is not a direct observation. They must learn the difference between 'fact' and 'opinion' before this drill can be considered complete.

'That lady is wearing a blue hat' could be considered to be a fact if it was observed. *'That person is a snob'* or *'That person is poor'* is an opinion, and not

necessarily a fact. There is a huge difference. Certainly the person may be a snob, and certainly they may be poor, but how can anyone conclude this to be a fact without speaking to the person and even then it could still be considered a fact. Frankly, all of these types of considerations are 'opinion', and not based in fact. Poor? *In relationship to what or whom?* Snobbish? *In comparison to what or whom?* It is all subjective.

Sales people too often get themselves into the trap of operating off of opinion about people and types of clients, rather than just looking at the *facts*. I can cite many examples where people who looked 'poor' walked into my showroom when I was in business there years ago and place surprisingly large orders for custom glass work, and paid in cash. I can also cite many examples of people who were well dressed who confided in me they were in bankruptcy and broke beyond broke. One cannot take opinions and operate with them as 'facts', nor can one pass judgment upon a person simply because of their appearance.

This is the important training discipline of this silent observation drill. Getting the sales person to recite factual observations, and not assumptive opinions about people is the focus of this drill. When they can cite factual observations with fifty consecutive people who walk by, you can feel confident that they have a grasp upon these points. They should be sternly corrected for any opinion they try to pass along as fact.

Let's take this even farther, and re-examine the

statement *'That lady is wearing a blue hat'.* This could at first glance be considered a fact, but is it? Did the sales person walk over and touch the hat? Is the hat blue all the way through or the same color on both sides, or is it another color on the other side which was away from the sales person's point of view? Is she in fact 'wearing a hat' or is it a 'bonnet'? Is the lady really or lady, or is it a man dressed as a lady?

You see that even a perceived fact could be examined closer, and it may turn out to have been an opinion after all. The important lesson in this drill is that one become finely tuned to what is factual in the world around them, and one should also be willing to re-examine the facts to make sure one is not operating with an *'opinion'* masquerading as a *'fact'*.

Real Time Drill #3
Direct Observation

There is a drill that is a good practical exercise for sales people to build up their confidence with speaking to the general public. One takes the sales trainee out to a public place where there are a lot of people, and instructs them to walk up to people and ask them a question.

The question should be benign like '*What do you notice about my appearance*' or '*What is best time of day to be at this park?*' while holding a clipboard as if doing a survey. Instead of writing down the person's answers, the sales person should instead be writing down 5-10 observations about each person they talk to.

What one is trying to accomplish with this drill is to get the sales person to *really look* at the person, and become familiar with the person they are speaking to. The best way to do this is the train in the discipline of *observing things* about the person.

What is important to stress in this drill is that they are not concentrating too much on writing when in front of the person, but instead they are *looking* and making a mental note of what they see. Then after the person walks away, write down their observations before approaching the next person.

In actual fact, between the first several interviews with live people, the sale manager should consult with the sales person, tell them not to look over at the person and then ask the following:

- *What did you observe about them?*

- *What color was their hair?*

- *What color were their eyes?*

- *What were they wearing?*

- *What color were their shoes?*

Each time vary the questions to details about the person he or she interviewed. The first few times they will pick up few details, but after repeated drilling they will begin to notice more and more. The sales managers questions should become more and more specific to see if the person can become tuned into more and more refined details the more they do the drill.

- *More refined questions such as:*

- *What colors were her earrings?*

- *What was the thread color on his tie?*

- *What did her perfume smell like?*

- *How many rings were they wearing?*

- *What was their accent?*

The more refined the details, the more interesting the drill becomes. You will be able to compare the notes they wrote down at the beginning of the drill to the ones towards the end and see that they have much more precise detail.

One should end the drill when the sales person demonstrates confidence in greeting people, talking to them and observing details about them. One should only end when the sales person also feels that they are confident that they can observe people and take note of details when they meet them.

This drill helps to develop a precise skill of observing details in other people they interact with, and in doing do they really begin to know the people and form a closer relationship with them than they ordinarily would. This can result in the sales person feeling more in control of their presentations as well.

Real Time Drill #4
Have You Seen My Elephant?

Take them out where there are large amounts of people outside of the showroom environment like a fair, mall or festival and accompany them. Have them walk up to people over and over again, introducing themselves.

Make then do it to complete strangers. After a few hours of this, they will start loosening up and relax with all kinds of people. You as a sales manager will also be able to see how they interact with all kinds of different people. Make note of the profiles of people they seem to back off from.

Are they intimidated by tall people, older people and single women? If you observe this or any such characteristic, have them confront people who fit that profile over and over again until they are comfortable. This can take some time with some trainees, but in the long run it is helping them acquire skills they need to work with people in the field of sales. They need to be able to speak to anyone, about anything, without backing off.

Next, If you really want to increase the gradient on this type of exercise, have them walk up to people over and over again and ask them a crazy question such as "*Excuse me, have you seen my elephant?*" as seriously as they can possibly deliver, and see how they deal with the reactions from people. This can also demonstrate to them that they can engage a complete stranger in conversation, if the communication is delivered smoothly. They will come to learn that it is not so much what they are saying to another in terms of words, but the affinity for the other person they demonstrate when they deliver the words the first time they meet them that matters.

This drill is to train a sales person to be comfortable asking anyone any question, no matter who they are, and open the door for them to control the conversation to arrive at a sale.

A sales person who can deal with all kinds of people from all kinds of background is the ideal, as well as one who is brave enough to ask the tough questions to get the information they need from the customer to sell them. If they can ask about a mysterious elephant bravely, then asking about a person's financial qualifications should be no cause to be nervous or have back off.

Real Time Drill #5
Signals from the Bench

Note: I have included this chapter here which was first published in '***The Art of Sales Management: Lessons Learned on the Fly***' because it has important information regarding this section on '*Real Time*' training for sales people. It is complete as the original time it was published.

৵৵৲

When one is working in a showroom environment, it can be a microcosm of a training ground. Customers walk in, sales people greet them, and they commence with presenting them the product. If they are successful they make a sale.

With training new sales people who are just getting used to this environment, it is helpful for them to have timely help from their sales manager when needed. Around the time that my business partners and I became owners of our company in the early 1990's, I was the only one experienced in selling the product. It was one of my first projects to train Karen, one of my new business partners in our approach to showroom sales.

Karen was a unique individual, as she had a lot of sales experience working with customers, so her only uncertainties lay with the product itself. It was somewhat of a challenge to be able to price custom artwork to begin with, but then to calculate the price in front of a customer, as well as answer individual questions about the installation, details, etc. becomes an even greater challenge.

So Karen wanted to have a means of letting me know when she felt she needed me to move in on the presentation, while she was engaged in it. However, I did not want to abruptly disrupt a presentation, if all was going well either. We needed a way for her to communicate with me when she needed me to make a timely move in on the presentation, without the customers being put at unease by it.

So being familiar with baseball, I presented the idea to her of creating a set of unique signals between her and me that would allow us to converse without the customers knowing it. I reference it now as the '*Signals from the Bench*' approach. Much like a baseball manager can signal information to a batter without the other team catching onto the message; I was proposing a similar system be adopted between her and me.

The way our showroom was positioned was with displays of products on the floor, specifically doors and windows. There was also a desk to sit down at with photo albums, samples, etc. after one was through showing the customer around.

The desk was positioned in such a way, that the customers would be facing the sales person and behind the salesperson was a wall with a display. The customers backs would be to the rest of the showroom, and this gave others freedom to move around without distracting the presentation at this desk. Also, as a manager, I could at any time walk into the showroom, and be behind them, and the customers would never be distracted by my presence.

So the signals Karen and I developed were simple. I could walk into the room behind the customers, and signal to her when she was in front of them. She would respond back with a signal letting me know what was going on. I would ask one question, and she would respond with one of three possible responses that we had also developed signals to represent.

For example: I would walk into the showroom look at her, make eye contact and visibly stroke my chin. This meant "*How are you doing?*" She would respond with one of the following:

A. Touching her nose - which meant '*No problem, I am okay*'. So she or I would not forget the sign, the 'no' in 'nose' was the reminder for '*No problems*'.

B. Passing her hand though her hair over the top of her head - This meant '*I'm in trouble, Help!*', and needed me to find a way to come in on the presentation she was doing immediately, and help her get it back on the rails or take over. The 'H' in 'Hair' and '*Head*' was a reminder of '*Help*', once again, so we had a reminder as to what the sign meant.

C. She would touch her right ear lobe or earring - This meant *'Stay Close'*, which meant that she felt like she was doing okay, but needed me to stay close just in case. The 'Ear' was a reminder for us both of *'Stay here'*.

These may sound very silly, but these 'signals' worked fabulously. She was able to tell me the status of things, without the customers having a clue about our conversation, and seamlessly carry on with her presentation. The simplicity of it was that it gave her control to call for help, or continue on, and I was not the one who needed to arbitrarily make that decision. The decision as to whether I came into the presentation at all was entirely up to her.

Over time we developed a few more specific signs, such as quickly making a 'T' shape with her fingers when the customer was looking away. This meant: *'Take Over'* for use when she had another client walk in that she needed to see, and the present person she was working with was just looking, etc. In those cases I would come over, and tell her that someone was there that needed to see her, and she would smoothly transition the people over to me by introducing them, etc.

Hand signals work great on the showroom floor with new and old sales people alike, and are in fact a lot of fun. There were many that we developed over time, and we would laugh about them later on as time progressed.

We also developed signals to communicate things that required no response, such as: *'Sit up straight'* when they were slouching, *'Look them in the eyes'* when they were avoiding eye contact, and simply *'say something'* when we observed their customer was merely looking at the photo albums and not really telling them anything, or realizing the salesperson was there.

Signals like this were used to assist the sale in progress, and help remind the salesperson they were in control. They were used for instructional purposes during live presentations, and followed up with coaching later if needed after the customers were gone. We never verbally interrupted a salesperson with these things while in front of a customer.

As a sales manager, I also developed some signals to use over the phone when a salesperson would call me when either I was out of the office, or they were at an appointment. These too were subtle, and simple. They let me know as a manager what the salesperson was working with, without the customer they were sitting across from them within earshot hearing or catching onto the coded message.

For Example: If they called me and said *"Hello, Michael? I'm here with (customer's name) and they want to know..."* The code in this was *'I'm here with'* followed by a name. This meant that they had a deal working and were close to closing it, but needed an incentive from me to make it final, or get them to commit.

Usually the name was given also because they knew I was familiar with that deal they were working, and the size of the order, etc.

I would then ask them to say 'yes' if they needed a discount, guaranteed install date, or needed me to come over, etc. until they would respond. When they would say 'Yes' and I would tell them what we could do, I usually did not know much more about what they were dealing with, but I trusted in their judgment, so most of these calls were resolved without me ever having to get involved first hand with the customer.

If they called and said *'Michael, I have a question. Can we _____'* That meant they had a client in front of them and they needed to call the sales manager to ask a question, for appearances only, and really did not need help and had things under control. The key phrase in this was *'I have a question'*.

One can develop any number of subjects, coaching tips, or reminders needed to communicate, and make a smooth selling environment. It also improves customer service by making the salesperson not have to stop what they are doing to go ask a question, or call for help when they need it. It gives them a chance to remain in control, and learn from the experience. They of course have the choice to call over help subtly, or carry on and weather through it as well.

Just like in professional sports, no player ever wants to come out of a game. To do this is to invite replacement, demotion or demonstrate incompetence in the field of play. Therefore, through the use of signals, it allows them to retain control over their presentation, and at the same time allow them to call in for help if they need it.

Whenever I was ever called into help after getting such a signal, I always turned control back over to the salesperson to carry on as soon as the matter was resolved. I never 'took over' as so many sales managers can be tempted to do. My function was to move in, assist, and move out as swiftly and smoothly as possible without becoming a distraction or bypassing the authority of the salesperson in front of the customer.

My operating basis on this was always understood by all my salespeople, so they never expected me to take over if called in. That is unless they sent me the signal for 'take over' as described earlier, and in those circumstances, I did so.

So there are many ways, like a baseball manager that a sales manager can communicate with your sales people while they are in action, and the customer is not distracted and you in turn can help them out. *'Signals from the bench'* is a great way to do this. It can be an invaluable tool to use with your team, as long as you practice it in advance, and all who are on your team know them cold. Thus if such a system is put in place, it should be drilled frequently. Sales meetings and one-on-one training sessions are a great way place to do this.

Showroom Drills

A showroom where clients walk in freely drawn in by marketing and advertising is a microcosm of a sales environment that requires a unique set of skills.

These prospective customers walking into such an environment inherently know they are walking into a nest of sales people. They know someone is going to try to sell them something, so quite often their defenses are up. It does not matter what their intention was in coming in. The most frequent response one will ever receive if you ask directly about their intention is '*Oh, I am just looking*'.

However, any experienced sales person knows that this is an automatic response which simply means 'I came in because I was interested, but please don't sell me something' or some other message. Seldom does anyone walk into a showroom of specialty goods just because they want to stimulate their optical nerves. They were driven there by desire and interest, no matter how slight.

Showroom sales success depends on the skills of a sales person who knows how to penetrate and engage a customer, and get them past this initial defensive mechanism and control the sales process. Showroom drills are about being in control of one's environment, and guiding a customer to make a purchase and help the customer fulfill their desires and interest.

The drills in this section help to develop the skills in a sales person who works in a showroom environment. The drills cover many basics that can enable a sales person to get past the 'elephant in the room' that the customer is trying to avoid confronting. This 'elephant in the room' is essentially *'I want to buy, but I am not sure if I should buy, but I need to be careful about being sold, etc.'*

It is a image of fear in the customer's own universe than must be driven out into the open gracefully, so that it become *'safe'* for the customer to make a purchase.

So in essence, a showroom sales person first target with any customer is to make the environment 'safe' for them to be in. This does not mean that one should leave them alone, which is quite often the illusion many sales managers fall into the belief of. No, the 'safe' environment is built upon friendly relations and interaction that places the customer at ease and makes them comfortable.

Comfort and security comes from a warm and friendly atmosphere, and this is what these drills seek to impart. That is the foundation of success in a showroom sales environment. To be successful in their application however, a sales person must first be comfortable in the showroom themselves.

Showroom Drill #1

Eight Corners Awareness

Sometimes one can have a sales person who is nervous about selling on a showroom floor. This can happen when they are new to a team, or just not used to walking up and talking to people face to face. Perhaps all of their prior sales work has been on the floor, or with people walking up to them at a trade show. One of the great ways to get them to settle down and focus is to use the drill of '8 Corners Awareness'.

This drill presumes there are 4 corners of the room where the ceiling meets the walls, and 4 corners of the room where the walls meet the floor. Have a sales person sit in a chair in the middle of the showroom before the business opens. Ask them to look at one corner of the room. Once they feel they have it located, and are comfortable looking at it, ask them to look at another corner. Take them through all 8 corners of the room without leaving their chair.

Once this is done, ask them to look forward and put their attention on two corners of the room at the same time. Once they are comfortable with two corners, have them focus on three, then four, etc. Do this until they can sit there and have attention and certainty with all eight corners of the room.

In doing this drill; they will develop a personal comfort in the space they are working. The showroom will become more comfortable to them, and they will be more at ease.

Doing a drill such as this can make them less nervous about dealing with customers who walk into the showroom. This drill can also be done with having them place attention on all four walls, the ceiling and floor at the same time. Work up to it on a gradient one by one. This drill helps to build personal stability in the showroom, and it helps to make the environment their own.

Showroom Drill #2
Five 'Elephant in the Room' Drills

In a showroom, being of a frame of mind where you are willing to engage a person in conversation and 'wake them up' is essential. Sometimes people are caught up in their own little world, and fail to see the world around them.

They appear to be there, but are somehow asleep on their feet and *out of touch* with the environment around them. It is important for you to get them to see your products, and think well of them.

There are five drills that one can teach a sales person to use that can wake someone up and compel them to engage the sales person in conversation if one applies them when they either walk in or shortly after.

I call these drills 'the elephant in the room' drills. Have you ever been in a group of people where no one is saying anything or getting to the point of why they are there? Everyone is avoiding the obvious, much like the old adage of the 'elephant in the room' where everyone sees it, but no one wants to be the first to mention it for fear of being embarrassed.

A sales person needs to be free from the reaction of 'embarrassment' and needs to be brave enough to say anything. This way they can be in control of their showroom environment. Here are the basic five 'elephant in the room' drills I suggest to use as a starter:

Say what you *see*

This was essentially 'looking at the person' who walked in, and follow it up with saying whatever you can about what you see before you. If a man walked in and was wearing a Braves hat, I would say loudly *'Look out we have a Braves fan!'* and the person would smile and engage in conversation. If a woman walked in with a purple dress *'Well, someone is looking purple today!'* and she would usually say something and engage in conversation.

State the Obvious

This was a little more of an observation of the person mood, and way they walked into the place. This was something you learned from observing. Men would walk in and appear to be looking at stuff, and but more like wandering. So I or my partner would say *'Well, let's see your wife is down at the quilt shop so you had to escape from that didn't you?'* and they would usually chuckle and begin talking about the doors, or engaging in conversation, etc. A woman would walk in alone and we would say *'It is okay, your husband is not here!'* We would get a laugh and a conversation.

Proclaim the Outrageous

The showroom would be full of people, and I would shout out *'Ladies and Gentlemen, don't anyone leave until you buy a lamp!'* or *'Folks, your mothers just called and she wants you to bring home a stained glass lamp. Might as well add it to your shopping list!'* or some other crazy thing that came to mind at the moment. The effect was a group of people lightening up, and even talking to each other, and their own comfort barriers would relax and amazingly enough they would start lining up at the cash register holding our products and buying. The *elephant in the room* is identified and exposed, and they are put at ease to buy.

Greet with Life

Whenever anyone walks in, greet them effusively. Walk up to them and make them feel that they are a long lost friend that you have not seen in forever. It is greeting people with 'life energy' and making sure the warmth and sincerity is conveyed to them. Make them feel welcome. If done correctly it can shatter any social barrier and put them at ease.

Tell them it is okay to buy

It may sound simple, but it works. When talking to someone about a product on the showroom floor, after you have pitched them the product and shown them around, turn to them and look them in the eye and say *'It's okay to buy it now'.*

You can also just say with sincerity *'It is really okay with me if you buy this right now.'* Say it with levity and warmth. Really mean it, and even follow it up with a motion to the desk to have them sign the papers. Sometimes this simple and direct approach is what the customer is waiting for, whether they are aware of it or not, and it cuts through all the barriers. It bypasses all the 'social machinery' they having spinning in their heads on how they buy things, etc. It simply makes it easy, and painless. It yanks the 'elephant in the room' out in the open, sets the concerns aside and gracefully puts everyone at ease.

Training a sales person to master this simple approach can make the difference in sometimes as much as 50% of their sales on the showroom floor. It is that valuable. It can be adjusted for many situations, but essentially a sales person learns to inject this 'resolution' at the right moment in the sale and it tears down a buyers 'social barriers' and places them at ease about buying.

If you can get a salesperson to a level where they are willing to *say anything*, you can bring out that wit and humor that will make their life in sales a wonderful experience and they will grow into a brilliant and creative member of your team.

Getting them to practice these skills as a form of drilling and getting a team of sales people to work together on this and play along can create a fun atmosphere where people enjoy spending money in your business. They will also tell others about their experiences and in so doing so create good word of mouth.

Showroom Drill #3
Touchy-Feely

Another exercise you can have sales people practice and include in their presentations with customers is a lot of what is called 'touchy-feely'.

This drill consists of getting the customer to touch the product you are selling. If they can touch it, it become more real to them, and it also a great way for the salesperson to become comfortable with selling a product. Customers tend to brighten up the more they can touch the product, and this will make sales easier and the sales person will become more comfortable too.

Salespeople in the car business use this method a lot. Getting the person to touch the car, turn the handles, sit behind the wheel is all part of that 'touchy-feely' drill. When I sold mahogany, oak and ash doors, I used to ask people to feel the wood all the time. It made them really connect with the product, and when I was starting out in sales and did not know all the finer details of the products yet, I certainly could just tell some to touch that door, or brass handle, etc. It made selling it so much easier once the customer was in physical contact with the product. It begins to build a sense of personal 'ownership' with a prospective buyer.

What one does to train a salesperson with this drill is to have them walk around with you as a sales manager or other sales people and touch the products. Ask them to explain the feel of the different surfaces to you, and ask them also about temperature, texture, etc. Get them to describe it to you with details and first impressions.

Ask them to use those same descriptions with customers, and train them to challenge customers to touch the products over and over again. Take the sales person around the showroom and have them touch the products over and over again until they are bright and happy with talking about the products, and are comfortable with moving around the showroom.

Then ask them to walk another sales person around and ask them to instruct the other sales person to touch each product over and over again, walking them around the showroom. Keep this up until the new sales person has a confidence that they can ask others to touch the products, and are certain that they can use this smoothly in their presentations to customers.

The result you are looking for with this drill is a new sales person who is completely uninhibited about walking around the showroom and touching products, and willing and able to ask the client to touch the products as a part of their presentation on the showroom floor.

By training your people to place the client in physical contact with the products one is helping them use a vital tool to raise a customer's sense of ownership for the products making it easier for them to buy. As a side note, the absolute worst sign anyone could post in a showroom is *'Do Not Touch'* which becomes quite obvious once one discovers the benefits of using this technique.

Showroom Drill #4
Move the Customer Around

There is a very precise set of skills that a sales person needs to master when working with sales on a showroom floor or on a lot showing products. This skill is being able to *move the customer around.* Standing and talking to a new prospect in a stationary position or location in the showroom can reduce your chances of a sale.

When a prospect walks in to see your products, show them one close by. Converse with them, and say *'Oh, let me show you this other one!'* or something similar and take off walking in the direction of that other product, and the customer will follow. It does not matter what you show them, what it important is that you show them something in another part of the showroom or your place of business. *Why?* This is because as a person moves around a space, they become familiar with it and will move more freely themselves around in it.

Have you ever been to a hotel where you are going to stay at for a few days? If you simply stay in your hotel room that is really all you know about the hotel and in your universe unconsciously that is the size of the space.

However, if you move about the hotel and visit the amenities, such as the pool, weight room, gift shop, etc. you will suddenly become oriented to the hotel, and can move about it more freely. Have you ever heard of people who have taken their kids to a hotel and learned that after the first few hours the kids are leading their parents about the hotel showing them the amenities?

The reason this happens is because as one moves about a new unfamiliar space, and learns things about it, the space becomes familiar. The more familiar it is, the more comfortable one is in the space, and the more relaxed one become. In sales using a showroom floor, it is essential to success to move the clients around the showroom floor. This is partly to show the variety of items, but subconsciously you are working to expand the space they client is in and in turn make them more familiar with the environment.

When a sales person is moving them around, they also are to a greater or lesser degree controlling the person. They are taking them back and forth to get them to compare the two products, and telling them to follow them. The customers follow them, and are subconsciously giving into a form of control by the sales person. This is the first step in getting them to be able to buy.

So in drilling a new sales person on a showroom floor, one needs to teach them the skills of being able to move the customer around. The basic sequence of the drill they need to learn follows a basic pattern such as this:

1) Greet customer who has walked in and is

looking at a product on the floor.

2) Talk to them about the product before them, and ask them questions, engage them in conversation, etc.

3) At some point say '*Oh, let me show you this other_____ here in our showroom, which I think you will like...*' and walk away in the direction of the product. Beckon the customer to follow if needed.

4) Once at the location of the new product, show them something about it, invite them to touch it, etc.

5) Then after a few minutes of touching it, say '*Now, let's go back to that first one and I want to show you something to compare about this one...*' and once again start walking and beckon them as needed.

6) Once back at the former product, show them something else about it. Invite them again to touch it.

7) After a few minutes, say '*Now that you have seen this, let me show you this other one...*' smiling and walk away, and beckon as needed.

8) Move the customer around back and forth to points they are now familiar with, and to new points. Show them products and differences of course, but this is secondary. What is primary is that one understands that they are controlling the customer and expanding their space, and in turn helping them to relax so they can be sold.

It works, and just moving a person around back and forth can be magical. A customer will suddenly say, *'You know, I like that one, but I think I want to buy the first one we saw when we walked in...'* This is music to a sales person's ears! You do not care which one they like, just that they like one and want to buy it!

What is important for a sales manager to understand is that the showroom needs to be set up so that there is space to move a person around, and that similar products are spaced far enough apart or in difference show rooms, etc. This way there can be some distance in which to move about, and ultimately expand a customer's space. The larger the space, the more comfortable they will become.

New trainees should be drilled on this technique and practice using other sales people. It can also be practiced in sales meetings, teaching the entire team. Moving the customer around is a very effective tool, and few sales people or sales managers who operate in showrooms realize its value.

This can be an effective tool to make any showroom a huge success, and it is so easy to train people to do. It is recommended as a first drill for sales people working in a showroom sales situation.

Working in a showroom can be so easy to let the products sell themselves simply by moving a person back and forth, to and fro around the showroom floor. It really is a magical dance.

Showroom Drill #5
Learn Five Things

One of the best showroom drills for sales people to practice is what is best described as the '*Learn Five Things'* drill. When one is working on a showroom floor, people walk in and inquire about products, financing, etc.

One can and should answer their questions, but if one is to really build a relationship with a person and help them overcome barriers on the road to owning your product, it works best to know something about them.

Therefore whenever one is training sales people in a showroom environment, one of the best drills to teach them is to '*Learn five things'* about your customer that you did not know'. The way to do this is through conversation, and asking questions. If you can learn five things about a person you can safely say you know a lot more about them than before they walked in.

It also give you a chance in the course of learning those five things to compare at least one of those five things to something you are familiar with and expand the conversation with them about that. This helps you move from being simply the '*unfamiliar sales person'* to becoming the '*friend in the _____ business'* with the customer.

Here are some things you might want to learn

about a customer. The best way to find these things out is to simply ask them:

- *Where are you from?*

- *Do you have any kids?*

- *Where do you work?*

- *Are you married?*

- *What is your favorite color?*

- *Are you new to the area?*

- *What brings you in today?*

- *What kinds of things do you like to do when you are not working?*

If you take some time, you can likely list out a number of other important questions you would like to know about the customer that you can ask directly or indirectly to gain a better understanding of them, and become that friend.

It is important to also note that in some professions like Real Estate, asking questions about familial status and marital status can be construed as a violation of the Fair Housing regulations (for example). So it is important to know the laws pertaining to your industry about what you can legally ask a client, and what questions you should avoid.

The basic concept behind '*Learn Five Things*' is

that it gives one an opportunity learn something about the customer, and become more familiar with them. It also opens doors for you to build a relationship with them as a friend, which is part of the magic of success in sales. Friends will return to buy from a friend again, and they will also refer to a friend. So making friends is what the drill of *'Learn Five Things'* is all about.

A sales manager can sort out any sales person who is losing sales on the showroom floor by asking whether they asked at least five questions. If they have not, then that can quite often be a point of correction. Drilling helps them practice the five question rule, and learn five things about their client.

It is something that should be practiced in role playing drills at sales meetings with all sales people periodically, even if they are previously trained in it. This is something that can often be forgotten, and sales people can get complacent on.

In sorting out a slump in sales, check if the sales people on the floor are *'learning five things'* about their customers, applying the *'touchy-feely'* drills, and *'moving the customer around the showroom floor'*.

These three drills combined make for a deadly set of basic strategies in showroom sales. If sales are declining it is quite often that one or more of these three has slid out of use, and needs to be gotten back in. These three are also the easiest techniques to teach new sales people to get them selling immediately.

Showroom Drill #6
Prep & Shift

A particular drill that can be used is the 'prep and shift' drill for training sales people on a showroom floor. Quite often in a showroom environment, new sales people can easily adapt to showing the product and answering questions about it, but do not necessarily have all their closing skills down yet.

Therefore a system can be put in place where the sales force is divided on the showroom floor of ones who prep a customer and ones who work out the financial side of a transaction and gets them to sign papers or '*close them*'.

Teaching a sales person the skill of 'prepping' and then knowing when a customer is reaching enough to buy and 'shifting' it is a skill that should be practiced with some drilling.

The best way to do this is to take some time in a role playing with the sales person on the showroom floor. Have them strictly focused on showing the product, and answering questions. Drill them so they have certainty. When they have this down then work with them on reading the customer for a close.

Get them to listen for certain important questions such as '*How much would this cost me installed?*' or '*Can you deliver?*' or 'What will be my cost to drive it off the lot?' etc.

Once they have this down and can recognize this point in the sales process, one then drills them on key lines to use to 'shift' the client smoothly without losing them to another person.

*"Let's go see what that would run... "*And then have the customer follow them to an office where they introduce them to a closer. Another way would be to just say *"Why don't we ask Dave?"* And walk them over to see 'Dave' or whoever is in that role.

Prepping and shifting to so it smoothly requires some drilling, and with some practice a new sales person can learn to be very effective at it. It is an extremely useful tool in showroom sales.

Speed Drills

Speed drills are used to instill and demonstrate the importance of teamwork. They do not necessarily reflect on practical application. In fact, they quite often are anything but practical, so can sometimes seem more of a fun exercise and it is easy to overlook the message.

Thus with the application of any speed drill, it is important to engage the group in discussion after the drill is completed to help guide them to the understanding of the importance of teamwork.

The discussion does not have to be of extreme length or very detailed. What is important is that group doing the drill and completing it gain an understanding that with teamwork they can accomplish more than as an individual effort.

The drills in this section are fast, and fun. They are easy to use with larger groups, and can make for a high spirited atmosphere. If one is looking to bring some life into a sales meeting or conference, then these drills will accomplish this for you.

The object of speed drills is to demonstrate not only the importance of teamwork, but also the importance of such practical concepts as 'coordination', 'cooperation' and 'organization'.

The drill formats vary, but all consist of involving members working together to perform a unified task. These drills can be used with any group activity, not just sales. They work for demonstrating and opening up discussion on how the many various departments of a company work together as a unified team. So if you are looking for drills to bring awareness to the concept of teamwork, speed drills are a great way to start.

Speed Drill #1
Pass the Book

There is a very easy drill that can be used to get the sense of speed and cooperative teamwork. The drill is called 'Pass the Book'. This is a simple one on the surface, but has a wonderful value as an educational tool on bringing about a greater understanding coordination.

Divide the group into two sections of 15-20 people each, and have them stand outside in a parking lot or other large conference space in two lines. These two teams will be competing against each other. Each should stand shoulder to shoulder, and have the two lines facing each other. A manager at one end would stand with a hardback book in hand and a stopwatch.

The discipline is to have each line pass the book to the person next to each other as rapidly as possible, and each person will have to have two hands on the book, and the person passing it has to say *'Here you are'* and the receiving person *'Thank you'* before the book can be released.

The idea is to have the book go all the way down the line as fast as possible, without violating the rules of *'Here you are'* and *'Thank you'* and each person having placed two hands on the book.

When the person on the end receives it, they are to hold the book over their head, turn around completely, and then pass it back up the line in the same fashion as before in the opposite direction. The drill is a test of time and accuracy. The group that can do it the fastest is the winner. This drill the first time through is always interesting, and there are always mistakes.

The discipline is to make it through without any mistakes, and be the faster team. If one only has a smaller group of say 10-15 people, then this drill can be done with one line, and the discipline is the beat the preceding time.

One will find that this is a lot of fun, and it is also a great ice breaker for getting a new group to work together and become familiar with each other.

Speed Drill #2
Deliver the Bear

Another variation of the prior speed drill is *'Deliver the Bear'*. This one is similar to the *'pass the book drill'*, but with a few differences. The teams are lined up as before, but with one major difference. They all stand shoulder to shoulder in a line, but every other person is facing the opposite direction.

Also, instead of a book, a stuffed bear (preferably a very large one) is used. The same *'Here you are'* and *'Thank you'* rules apply, but one must now deal with the turning of the shoulders in an opposite direction to pass the bear, and each team member must have two hands on the bear before and say *'Thank you'* before it can be released.

This is done timed in the same fashion as the other drill, and can be run over and over again to improve time. It adds a new level of coordination, and if anyone drops the bear the person at the front of the line must run and pick it up and run back to the start of the line and start over.

The drill is timed as before with the manager at the front handing off the bear and using a stop watch. Run the drill over and over until everyone is feeling good that they can accomplish it. One can also increase the difficulty on this by using a large beach ball, or some other challenging object to pass (use your imagination).

Speed Drill #3
Over & Under

Another speed drill is *'Over and Under'*. This drill is a new level of discipline. It requires lining up as in the other two drills, but each line is facing forward, single file. Instead of being close together like the above shoulder to shoulder drills, they are all an arm's length separated from the person in front of them.

A medium to large sized beach ball is used in this drill. The person at the front of the line receives the ball at the start of the drill from the manager who hands it off and starts the clock.

The first person passes it over their head to the person behind them saying 'Here you are', and the next person receives the ball with a 'Thank you' and then passes it between their legs to the person behind them, who in turn receives it in the same fashion and hands it over their head to the person behind them, and so forth.

The ball is passed over and under down the line, and the person at the end does a complete turnaround with the ball over their head and then passes it back up the line and it is returned over and under back to the start of the line and handed to the manager.

This requires a higher level of coordination, and once again if anyone drops the ball they must deliver it to front of the line and the drill starts over, etc. One can also run this one with the ball being passed down the line over everyone's head, hand to hand, and then at the end the last person in line passes it back between the legs to the person behind them, and it passes all the way back up the line under in the same fashion.

Speed Drill #4
Tie the String

Another speed drill that involves a group standing in line side by side working together as a group is 'Tie the String'. This drill can be done at a sales meeting or conference, and it consists of having the team stand in a line side by side. Each team member is given a piece of string of various lengths. They should be different types of string, yarn, cloth, etc.

At one end, the first person in line is handed a small rubber or plastic ball about the size of a baseball or softball. This first person is required to tie their string around the ball, and hand it to the next person in line when done, and they in turn tie their piece of string to the ball, and hand it off to the next person and so forth as it goes down the line.

This drill is timed, and can be run with two teams playing against each other for the best time. The object is to have the ball move all the way down the line with each team member adding on their contribution of a new string as it progresses down the line.

To increase difficulty one can run this drill with the following subtle changes each time:

A. Have each team member blind folded.

B. Have every other team member facing the opposite direction.

C. Make the requirement that the ball is passed behind each person's back, and they have to tie the string on behind their back, and when done pass it along.

D. Make the strings shorter as they go down the line, requiring more creativity to attach them to the ball.

E. Use a larger ball, and make each piece of string shorter than the circumference, requiring that every two team members in line have to work together to tie their strings together and then around the ball before passing is down the line.

F. Any combination of the above at the same time.

There are various ways to modify the drill to make it more challenging, and one can use imagination to get creative with it. What is important is that one creates a sense of spirit of working together for a common goal. This drill as it gets more difficult requires more and more teamwork and working together along with problem solving.

This can be a great ice breaker drill to use in an effort to get a team to work together for the first time, or just build friendship and cooperation. Separating a group into two or more groups playing against each other in this drill can be a lot of fun.

Speed Drill #5
Ball & Hoop

Another fun speed drill to help build comradeship and teamwork is the 'Ball and Hoop' Drill. This requires a beach ball and a child's plastic '*Hoola-Hoop*' (or it can be any large hoop that is big enough for a person to step through it easily). The ball should be big enough that it requires two hands to hold onto, and not so large that it cannot pass through the hoop.

The way this drill is run is to have your teams stand in a line, and the first person in the line is handed the ball. The second person is handed the hoop. When the clock starts, the first person in line must take the ball and with it in hand pass it through the hoop to the third person in line.

When the third person has the ball, the second person takes the hoop and passes it to the fourth person in line only they must not release it until the third person in line has stepped through the hoop with the ball.

When the third person has stepped through the hoop, they pass the ball through the hoop to the fifth person in line, and that person must in turn step through the hoop before the fourth person can pass the hoop to the sixth person in line.

This continues on down the line all the way to the end, and then when the last person in line has the ball the process reverses and goes back down the line.

This is a speed drill, and requires everyone on the team to work together to be the fastest. It requires thinking and coordination. It is a lot of fun and best run with larger groups. One can get as creative as they want with modifying the drill to make it more challenging.

If the drill is run a few times, and becomes too easy, try increasing the difficulty by making the following alterations:

A. Have the person who has the ball and steps through the hoop have to stop and sign their name on the ball before they can pass is to the next person.

B. Have the person who passes the hoop have to stop and tie a string onto the hoop before they can pass it along.

C. Add a second ball of a different size, and require the ball holder to have to pass both as well as step through the hoop with both.

D. Add a second ball of a different size and require the ball holder to have to pass one through the hoop and never let the other pass through the hoop, requiring more creative coordination to keep the one outside the hoop and one inside the hoop as it passes on down the line.

E. Have all the ball holders be blind folded.

F. Have each of the ball holders have their hands tied together.

This can be a fun and lively drill. It requires teamwork and a degree of problem solving to become faster and faster at it, thus it works best if you have two or more teams playing against each other.

Speed Drill #6
The Assembly Line

This drill has similarities to the sorting drill, but it is done with a group of sales people. One stands them in line, in front of a long table or bench. On that table or bench in front of them are parts that connect together. This can be a set of Lego blocks, or some sort of Velcro parts or pipe fittings, etc.

One person starts at the end of the line and attaches a piece to another piece, and hands it down to the next person who grabs a piece of an item in front of him or her, attaches it on, and hands it to the next person, etc. The idea is that the 'object' that they are building is random and grows larger as it passes down the line, making it more challenging to work with.

What one is trying to teach the team to do is to work together and solve problems, and create something together as a team. One can place two separate lines of sales people if there are larger groups and have them compete against each other against a clock. The first team done is the winner.

A finished product should include at least one part for every salesperson in the line when finished, and one should be able to hold the final creation up without is falling apart.

One can create even more challenging levels of skill with this drill by requiring that they build an item that can 'stand freely on its own in the end' or 'have only one supporting leg' etc. One can also require that they use no spoken words in the process, and complete the drill in silence or perhaps even blind folded for added levels of difficulty.

The idea is to get them to work together and contribute to a 'common creation' as a team, and accomplish a common goal. It is important after the fun of drill is over to engage them in discussion about what they can learn from working together as a team on this project, and whether or not they discovered anything that they can apply in terms of teamwork when working on group sales, etc.

You will be surprised on the insight they can gain on the subject of teamwork from this simple and fun drill. This can be used at a conference setting, or in a weekly sales meeting, etc.

Speed Drill #7
The Sorting Drill

This drill is essentially a skill builder for a sales person or team to help them develop understanding on how to prioritize paperwork. A sales manager who developed this drill explained it as follows:

One takes a mix of a large amount of old paperwork for orders for the products in the company. Include receipts, work orders, drawings, notes, sketches, phone notes, etc. Include also some random items that are not related to the files, such as newspaper clippings and illegible notes. Make the pile big enough to fill a large garbage bag and dump it on a table in front of the trainees.

Tell them first to sort the pile, and tell them they are on the clock for 30 minutes. Do not give them any instruction on how you want it sorted, or what any of the particles are. Just tell them to sort them and look blankly at them if they ask questions. Give them a 'Start' and stand back and wait for the 30 minutes to be completed.

What you are looking for as a manager is not whether they sort the pile. What is important is how they prioritize the particles. From observing them sort, one can learn what they place importance on, and how they sort particles that may come across their desk in the future. Once they are through this initial step of the drill, examine what they have done after you stop the clock.

Then get them to critique their own sorting. By doing so, they will often originate that they have misunderstandings on some of the paperwork, the value of certain items, etc. Answer their questions and sort them out on the papers. Then ask them to sort the pile again but for this time through the drill give them parameters such as 'sort them by customer name' or 'sort them by type of particle' etc.

Give them about 15-20 minutes on this last step until they are feeling good about it, and then stop the drill. Ask them to compare the first drill to the second one, and get their insight into what they learned about priorities in client files, types of papers, etc.

Once this is done, you can effectively give them common sense parameters to follow in regards to how they keep their client files organized, and sorted. It is a drill that can be modified to any activity.

It has a purpose to raise a person's awareness from seeing paperwork as a total random mix of particles, to being able to see the important pieces and priorities of particles in a client file or record system. It is a drill to improve understanding in regards to keeping good records to avoid chaos when one needs to go back and find something.

Speed Drill #8
Add Something

There is another speed drill that can be run to build a sense of urgency and team energy. It has to do with writing something to add to the copy of a brochure which has not been said about a product. It is a 'thinking on your feet' type of creativity required for this one.

One starts with group of sales people sitting in a circle, in chairs or standing, whichever you choose. Take a pad of paper and write on the top of the page one line of a product you are selling in your company. If it is automobiles, write at the top of the page *'Red 4 Door Sedan Model# ____'* or something similar, or whatever the product is.

Then one hands the pad of paper to the first person in the circle, ask them to write a one line description of the product that they would tell a customer. Give them an example such as *'Smooth riding'* or *'Automatic transmission'*, etc.

Once they have done this, have them hand it to the next person in the circle and have them add another description. Do this with a timer to create a sense of urgency. Each person should be handed the pad, read what is already written and they are then required to write a different description on the pad of the product. The drill is done when the pad passes 3 times around the room, or someone gets completely stumped on descriptive ideas.

This drill can best be done with two groups competing against each other, and the winner is the one who either has the most unique descriptions or completes the circle in full three times through. Points can be added for each description, and deducted for duplicate ones. The concept for this drill is to get them as a group with the silence of a written word to read and contribute to the description of the product as a team.

Speed Drill #9

Run to the Board

This drill consists of having a group of sales people sitting in chairs facing a white board that is placed approximately 10 feet in front of them. The drill is very simple. They are each given a slip of paper with ten things written down on it. The items on the list are to be kept secret from everyone else.

They are then instructed that one person will be handed a marker and told to run up to the board and write down the first item on their list, and then turn, run back to the group and hand off the marker to the next person who will then do the same.

This continues until every person has been to the board 10 times and written down each of their 10 items. There are several ways to make this interesting:

A. Have each of the items in sequence be related (such as all item number ones be colors, number twos be cars, etc.)

B. Have each word on the list be the words from a story, such as a chapter from 'Alice in Wonderland' or 'Peter Pan'. Each person would of course be required to run to the board in a sequence of 1,2,3,4,etc to make this story unfold and keep the group engaged in reading it as it goes along.

C. It can also be words that form a particular policy or writing within your organization, which becomes also a great way for the team to learn it and remember it in the future.

This is a fun and lively drill that is high energy, and can be run with one large group or two or more playing against each other. The drill should consist of requiring the sales people participating to run to the board, write down what they have to write and hand off the marker to the next salesperson much like a baton in track and field before returning quickly to their chair.

The constant movement makes it a very alive and energetic drill, and the fun factor creates the interest as a game.

Speed Drill #10
Write a Name

There is another fun speed drill that requires some thinking as well as coordination and teamwork. It is called 'Write a name'. The way this works is to have the team or a team standing in line and the first person on the end of the line is given a pad of paper and a pen.

The group is instructed that when a person has the pad, they are to turn to the person next to them who will turn around and let them use their back as a writing table.

The first person with the pad places the pad on the back of the person next to them and writes down a name of a person they know whose last name starts with the letter 'A' and then hands off the pad and pen to the next person in line who takes the pad, and does the same with the person behind them, only this time they write down the name of person they know whose last name starts with the letter 'B'.

This continues through the alphabet (skipping the letters X & Q if you want to). One can then have this run all the way to the end of the line, and then turn around and come back up the line ending at the original person who started the drill.

To increase difficulty as this drill is run; one can make any combination of the suggested changes:

A. Require each person write 2, 3, 4 or 5 names.

B. Require when they write a name, that they also write down three things about that person such as 'hair color', 'the car they drive', 'the school they went to', 'how many kids that person has', etc.

C. Require that each person has to spin the pad upside down from the person in front of them, and write their name upside down below the prior name on the list, and so forth.

D. Run the drill through the alphabet multiple times.

This drill can be created upon to enable people on your team to think faster on their feet, and it challenges their recall. It is a great one for conferences or just a skill sharpening drill at a weekly sales meeting. It is fun and lively, especially when done against the clock and teams playing against each other.

Conference Drills

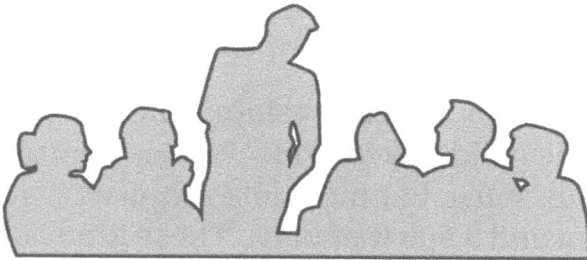

Conference drills are typically run with larger groups of people. They are designed to be used at sales conferences where large sales forces or groups of people in a similar sales profession are gathered to network, receive company-wide direction and learn skills.

These types of drills forward concepts such as the importance of *'teamwork'*, *'coordination'*, *'cooperation'*, *'friendship'*, *'understanding others'*, *'games'*, *'organization'* and *'unity'*. There can be many other valuable messages conveyed and discovered from executing such drills, and they serve as a platform for great follow-up discussion in any conference setting.

These drills are typically fun activities that can range from the simple to the very complex. They quite often require the use of props, materials and groups of people in order to execute them. They also can be implemented indoors or outdoors, and both types are included in this section.

The primary theme that runs through such large group practical drills is that they have a message of some kind that all members can gain a benefit from receiving, new or experienced alike.

These drills are entertaining and can quite often bring out the child in everyone. Some require an adventurous spirit, but most just require creative enthusiasm and a spirit of play. These kinds of drill break the monotony of a boring conference, and quickly become the memorable fun memories for those who attend.

Some are more elaborate than others and the set up and preparation time to put on such drills will vary. Everyone will have fun with these nonetheless. It is important to always include some sort of group discussion following such drills to discover what members learned from the drill; even if it is just that they had a fun time doing it.

The messages learned do not have to be profound, what is most essential is that participants leave with a greater feeling of teamwork, friendship and unity.

The important thing to remember about any conference or drills one implements is that they should not be too cluttered on the schedule, nor should they be boring.

Too often sales conferences become a dumping ground for information on sales people, and fail to introduce inspiration. The drills presented in this section vary on different levels of creativity, and most have been used at a variety of different sales conferences around the globe.

Not every drill will work for every organization. One should consider this section as a resource for ideas which can be modified to suit a conference or sales meeting.

It is unrealistic to expect a 'one size fits all' drill or practical exercise for every organization or company, however one can borrow and change any of these drills to make it work, or use them solely as inspiration to create your own ideas for injecting energy into your next conference.

Have fun planning your next conference with them!

Conference Drills 1 – 10
Conference Drill #1: Minefield

Building trust among members of a sales team, including members who may have 'trust issues', can help bring cohesiveness to the sales force as a whole. One great team-building activity is called "mine field" which is a game to help sales representatives learn to trust each other.

This can be an important variable when working together to close a sale. The set up for this requires that various obstacles, like chairs, box or cones should be placed randomly around a large indoor or outdoor space, leaving enough room for a person to walk through.

Divide sales team members into pairs in which one person is blindfolded and given verbal instructions to walk through the space while the others give instructions to turn right, left, stop, back up and turn around while they navigate the 'mine' field with the coaching of their friends.

This can become a fun and exciting contest when played between two or more teams at the same time at a conference.

Note: If two or more teams are playing in close proximity. the commands shouted out by each team may cause some additional chaos that can make the event more challenging.

Conference Drill #2: Product Pipeline

This conference drill is an interactive business simulation which encourages sales people to work together within smaller group, as well as within the larger mock "company." Two 'companies' are formed and grouped into smaller teams. Each small team or "department" of 5 to 10 people works in a 10'x 10' area that is connected to the working areas of the other teams in the conference room where it is held.

The "departments" must use limited supplies (plastic pipe, balloons, bamboo shoots or stakes, rubber bands, marbles, cups, etc.) to create a device that will transport or move a maximum number of marbles across a specified distance safely.

The challenge is that each team's section of the pipeline must interface and interconnect with those before and after it created by other teams. Two project managers that you elect oversee the project are challenged to make sure the 'company' meets the needs of the customers.

The different department's individual pipelines have a minimum marble "revenue" requirement to meet. Pipeline departments also have a budget that they can spend at a "store" for select purchases of materials. Different rules can be set up for how this works.

The separate companies marketing departments

must present a wonderfully creative presentation for the pipeline product before the final moment of truth. There is also an opportunity to perform more than one round of marble delivery to examine best practices and process improvement. A diversity of roles means a chance for everyone to be included. Time is limited. Which company will come in under budget, communicate effectively and meet their goals?

This conference drill can be quite an exciting undertaking and a lot of fun for all involved, as well as bring a greater understanding of how a company works from end to end. This can be a great drill for bringing awareness of teamwork at a conference.

Conference Drill #3: Chili Cook Off

Pooling teams together to make competing batches of chili at a conference can be a new and exciting project for all in attendance. Start the conference early in the day and separate the participants into teams of 6 to 8, and give each group a crock pot and some basic common ingredients like beans and butter.

Place a central table in the middle of the room with ingredients for all to use. Include beans, peppers, chili powder, meats, onions a multitude of other ingredients accessible to all teams to use. Have all teams review the available ingredients, and reveal to them the awards available and let them formulate a plan of what their batch of chili should be like.

Let all the groups use their creative juices to come up with the perfect batch of chili. Have them start the cooking early in the day, and have everyone share in the chili later in the afternoon and set up a judge's panel. Award first, second and third place awards to the winning groups or perhaps compartment the awards into 'most spicy', 'most sweet' and 'best overall', etc.

Whatever the award system you use, the magic is in the cooperative efforts of the individual teams to work together and devise their best recipe.

Conference Drill #4: Chocolate Bridge Building

Remember '*Willy Wonka and the Chocolate Factory*'? Imagine Charlie knowing he has trouble in the chocolate factory, and needs to build a bridge over the troubled chocolate waters.

This conference drill consists of pure imagination and design. Separate the participants into competing teams, and give them all the same supplies of chocolate bars, Popsicle sticks, gum drops, etc. Give them a task to build a bridge across a pan of water equal in size and distributed to each team. Cut them loose, and let the magic begin! Arrange for a panel of judges to choose the winners.

Conference Drill #5: Selling a quill pen to William Shakespeare

The game is called '*Selling a quill pen to William Shakespeare*' where the delegates are set the challenge of selling a writing quill to William Shakespeare. The brief asks them to think about what questions they will need to ask, the benefits to William Shakespeare of owning a quill and any objections they may need to overcome. There are several variations to this game.

Allow the delegates around 15 minutes to prepare their presentation which must involve every member of the group and the presentation should last no longer than 5 minutes. The delegates then present their sales presentation to William Shakespeare who is normally played by the sales manager or sales trainer. The winner is selected by the sales manager or trainer for whichever group comes up with the best pitch or presentation. Will the sale of the quill pen 'be' or is it 'not to be?'... That is the question!

Conference Drill #6: Tower of Chocolate

Similar rules apply here as the earlier conference drill on bridge building. Teams separate and build competing towers of chocolate using the same quantity of materials. The winners are chosen for tallest and most aesthetic. The ultimate goal is cooperation and team work in building a common project.

Conference Drill #7: Highest Pumpkin

A conference drill requiring teams to utilize folding chairs to build a tower. Each team is given a pumpkin and the same quantity of folding chairs (and sometimes tables) to use for their structure. The object is to use the resources they have to build the tallest tower structure and have the highest pumpkin from the ground. When all the towers are built, the judge come around with a step ladder and measuring tape and the tallest structure measured is the winner. This drill can be done indoors or outdoors, and creates a fun atmosphere of teamwork.

Conference Drill #8: Build a Tee Pee

Similar in set up to the prior drill, except teams are given a supply of PVC pipes, broom sticks and twine. Each team is given also a flag. The competition consists of giving each team the same allotted amount of time (say 20 - 30 minutes) to devise a plan and build a Tee Pee structure and hoist their team flag on the top of it. This is a thought provoking and challenging activity as each team must balance the strategy of planning and building with a goal of having the highest Tee Pee of all. The winner is measured and whichever team has the tallest Tee Pee wins.

Conference Drill #9: Sand Castle Building

If you are fortunate to have a conference that is near a beach, then this might be a great team building competition to put on as a conference drill. Give each team a similar allotted time, with castle building tools like shovels, trowels, buckets and cups and let them create together in similar roped off areas along a beach. The winning team is the one judged with the best sand castle and awards are given also for creativity, originality and humor.

Conference Drill #10: Boat Building

Another great outdoor conference drill for the summer time is to provide each team the same materials of rubber ducks, inflatable donuts, Styrofoam, tubing, rope and cloth. The challenge for this event is to build a boat that can transport one of their team members across a small pond or river. The first team to successfully do it wins. This can be a great activity for building teamwork and it gets everyone outdoors enjoying the sunshine and water.

Conference Drills 11 – 20

Conference Drill #11: Ginger Bread House Building

This is similar to the other drills requiring the building of a food structure. Only this time it requires the building of a ginger bread house by the individual teams as they compete against each other for the best looking and creative abode.

Like the drills that are similar to this one, each team is given the same quantity of materials and are given a space to build their structure, as well as an agreed upon allotted time frame. Each team is required to choose an architect from among their group and a builder.

The architect is required to design the ginger bread house, but may not partake in the building. However, they are required to coach the team members to follow the plans through the builder. The builder is the member of the group that coordinated the other team members to follow the instructions, and may partake in the construction although all members must be allowed to participate equally as possible.

Conference Drill #12: Scavenger Hunt

A scavenger hunt can be a great cooperative team challenge event for a conference. It is best done in a area where the conference is being held in a hotel near a shopping district, downtown area or perhaps even a casino. The teams are organized and given a list of approximate 100 odd items ranging from the obscure to the common. They are given one hour or similar time frame.

The team that goes out and collects the most items on the list is the winner. The only restriction is that they cannot purchase the items on the list. They must obtain them by any means of persuasion to gather the items on the list. This can be an extremely fun and challenging activity for a group of sales people at a conference to engage in and it is a great way to build bridges of communication between members attending, and create a sense of teamwork.

Conference Drill #13: Charity Team Participation

A great way to involve a team of sales people with the community is to have them participate in some sort of community charity activity. Food banks are great charities to have them participate as a group. Quite often they have programs for volunteers to bag food for charity, or make deliveries to the community, or some other task.

These kinds of activities can be both fulfilling and rewarding, and can build a sense of teamwork and connection to the community.

Conference Drill #14: Picture This

Team members have some of the information but can they communicate what they know? Who will see the big picture?

Each person gets images that are part of a larger sequence. Even though members are in different parts of the room, the group must decipher the sequence without any person seeing anyone else's images while the clock ticks! Will the group see the big picture in time or will they get bogged down in details...or worse yet, fail to notice a crucial part of the image in time? This complex verbal communication skill builder has a powerful "a-ha" factor that makes the grand unveiling unforgettable! This drill can be used at a live conference or online with members meeting in cyberspace.

Conference Drill #15: Catapult Building

Each team is given a variety of miscellaneous parts. Broom handles, rope, a chair and as many other parts as the event organizers can gather together to make the event interesting. Teams are given a time frame to construct a catapult that can toss a Teddy Bear across the room into a basket. The winning team is the one that can either toss the bear using the catapult before a time limit, or the when all teams are completed, the one that can toss it the greatest distance. This can be a fun cooperative team action game to make it a challenge and it provides some great entertainment.

Conference Drill #16: Find 'Stimpy'

Suppose you are holding a sales conference where there is a lot of material that is being covered, and one is issuing a conference brochure or manual as a training tool.

What would be a way to be sure your sales force pours through the material in detail? Or at least looks closely at every page?

There is a game called '*Find Stimpy*' where one hides a little image of a cartoon character within the pages. For an interesting conference, try hiding ten images of '*Stimpy the fish*' throughout the brochure. Hide him in an article, photo, advertisement, product description, etc. Have him upside down, sideways, black and white, multi-colored, large and small.

Announce on the first day of the conference that you are holding a drawing for a $500 Visa Gift Card (can also be cash or something similar), and to qualify for it all one has to do is fill out a card that identifies on what pages and where on the page '*Stimpy the fish*' is located in the manual.

Make it known that everyone should seek to find it on their own, and not share the locations in the brochure with others in order to improve the odds of winning. This kind of contest also offers a great way to sell advertising to the suppliers of products a company might sell to be sure that all the ads are inspected and looked at by the sales force during the conference.

Conference Drill #17: Free Throws

A simple conference drill for a low budget sales training session is to take the entire sales conference to an indoor or even outdoor basketball court. Hold a free throw contest after grouping them into teams. Give each team a maximum number of attempts at free throws, say 25 each team.

Make it a requirement that every team member throw at least one shot, and let the rest of the team work out a strategy to distribute the other shots among each other. This will require that they really get to know each other at least on the subject of sports, so that can make the best decision on who should get the lion's share of the remaining shots.

Increase the competitiveness by awarding a prize like a T-shirt for the winner, and also individual prizes for the sales person who makes the most baskets. This can be a fun event to build upon and make the conference interesting, and it does not require a lot of set up or equipment, just a ball and a basketball hoop.

Conference Drill #18: Egg Drop Challenge

This drill can be an interesting *'group against*

group' challenge, and it is quite definitive in its outcome. Divide your group into teams of 3, 4 or 5. Give them materials such as a 2 inch square piece of bubble wrap, Popsicle sticks, masking tape, celery sticks, paper clips, pencils, chewing gum, rubber bands, Crete paper, tooth picks and a raw egg.

One can vary the materials and use some creativity. Instruct each team that they must build a safety harness for their egg that would allow it to survive a 10 foot drop from a step ladder. Let each team build their contraption together using their own imagination, and allow them a time limit to do so (20-30 minutes).

When the time is up, the eggs and their respective devices are delivered to the front of the room where the master of ceremonies will take each egg and contraption and climb up a 10 foot step ladder and drop the egg + device from an equal distance onto a hard surface.

This can be made fun with music such as a drum roll, and photographers, etc. The teams whose eggs survive without a crack are the winners and are awarded a prize for each member.

The prizes do not have to be complicated of expensive. They could be a spatula, egg beater, a T-Shirt or a gift certificate. Use your imagination. This is a fun and entertaining drill, and can get a little messy with some broken eggs, but overall everyone will enjoy playing along with it.

It offers a fun opportunity for participants to get to know each other, collaborate on a small project and experience a sense of competitive team work.

Conference Drill #19: Inspirational Graffiti

This is a drill that can be done through the entire time frame of a conference. This one usually works best for a larger conference. In the meeting hall where the conference is being held, tape up large white banners of paper on the walls around the room. Label each banner with a number for a topic (topic #1, topic #2, etc.)

Throughout the conference hold several sessions which require the teams to do brain storming sessions on the a variety of topics such as 'the perfect introductory greeting with a new customer', 'The best one line inspirational quote they have ever heard', 'The best shopper stopper line', 'The best closing line', etc. After each session ask the various teams to have one member go to the banner on the walls and write down their team's contribution on each topic on the respective banners.

Before the close of the conference, have digital photos taken of each of the banners and make them available for all who have attended on a website or email, etc. One can also have someone transcribe them all into a single brochure, and give each member a copy as they leave.

The collaborative effort of the attendees can offer some very inspirational and valuable information to motivate all who attended even when they have left the conference.

Conference Drill #20: Write a letter to yourself

This is a drill that makes for a lot of interesting reflection. It has three parts. First the attendees are each given paper to write on. They are asked to write a letter to themselves from their viewpoint now, with all their experiences they have learned. Tell them to write the letter to themselves as if they were receiving it when they were twelve years old.

What would they say to themselves on what to do in life? What advice would they impart? What people would they recommend they avoid? What different roads would they suggest? Give them time to do this drill, and when they are done ask a few of them to volunteer and share their letters with the group. Once everyone has had some insight into this, and heard the results from others, move onto the next step of the drill.

The next step is to ask them to write a letter to themselves now, and what they would want themselves to know about how they are doing, what they have enjoyed about the road they have traveled so far, etc. Give them time to write this letter, and then repeat as in step number one. Ask for volunteers to read their letter or parts of it to the group. Open some discussion on this for a few moments, and then move onto the final step.

In the final step ask them to write a list of goals they would like to achieve in five years. Then have them write a letter to themselves which they will read five years from now, and what they would like to tell themselves about those goals and how they did. Have them seal the list of goals and the letter in an envelope, and address it to themselves and hand it to the front of the conference room. Tell them all that someone in charge of the conference will make sure that the letters are mailed back to them five years from now.

This can be an inspirational and insightful drill, and open the doors to some great discussion about goals, decisions and experiences that have been positive and beneficial. It is important for whoever is directing this drill to emphasize the positive in this last step, and encourage them to paint a brighter future for themselves.

When the attendees leave the conference, the sales manager or coordinator should take each envelope to be mailed in 5 years and insert them into another envelope and mail them to the individuals upon their return home one week or one month after the conference.

Before sealing the envelope, write in red on the outside "Open me in on (insert date). Store this in a safe place until then." Then mail the letters. The reason one should do this is that it can be very difficult to wait 5 years and expect it to be mailed, and also some members may want to open it a week later and review what they wrote.

This drill can be modified as one chooses. The future date could be set for one year from the conference, which would make it easier to coordinate a mailing. It might also be something that can be sent to them along with the invite for the next year's conference. There are many ways this can be varied. What is important is that one gets the attendees thinking in terms of future goals and targets they want to achieve, and give them a chance to challenge themselves to meet them.

Summary of Conference Drills

Conference drills should focus on developing skills, building team work, setting goals, collaboration and bringing a group together as a working family. The conference drills provided in this section are by far not all that can possibly exist, and there are many, many more that can be created to keep sales conferences and meetings fresh and exciting.

These presented here can offer some fodder for future creation, and all have been tested and run with success at various conferences for different companies. A sales manager or trainer is often called upon to keep the group inspired and enthusiastic, as well as productive in their efforts at selling.

Conference drills can be a fun and exciting way to do this.

Summary

The application of drills can help to develop skills on many levels. Some of the important themes presented in this book include the building of teamwork and cooperation. Drills also inspire creativity and imagination, and encourage the increase of one's skills.

They challenge participants to discover new methods, develop new ideas on how to resolve problems and also learn new ways of doing things. Some of the drills presented here can also show a sales person their own unique blind spots on areas that they never knew they were having trouble with.

All in all, the application of drilling opens new doors, and helps to develop skills with new and experiences sales people alike. They are a valuable tool for any sales manager or sales trainer to use, and this book was designed to approach the subject of sales training from many new directions and present challenges on different levels.

If you have gotten to this point in this book, hopefully you have found some inspiration along the way or perhaps a new tool or two that you will endeavor apply to their own job in working with others.

Many of the drills presented here transcend many professions, and can be applied to more than just the sales person. They can be applied or adjusted for a multitude of industries that are seeking to bring their personnel together as a team and achieve excellence. The reader is hereby encouraged to apply the material contained herein, and also adjust it as needed to their own unique sphere of influence.

As an author and former sales manager, I hope you have enjoyed this book and would encourage you to read my other books in this series: '**The Art of Sales Management: Lesson Learned on the Fly'** and '**The Art of Sales Management: Revelations of a Goal Maker'.**

I wish you the greatest prosperity in any activity that you are a part of. The journey of infinite possibility begins here.

Enjoy the ride!

About the Author

    Michael Delaware is a Phoenix, Arizona native who now resides in Battle Creek, Michigan with his wife Margarita. He also lived in Georgia for 15 years in the 1980's and 1990's where he owned and operated a stained and beveled glass studio in the Metro-Atlanta area. During those years he was an active volunteer in the community, coordinating annual Arts and Crafts Festivals in the downtown district of Roswell, Georgia. He also participated in Arts & Crafts Shows for over 25 years as a vendor in numerous States. He has been a Michigan resident since 1999.

    His other published works include numerous

non-fiction books on real estate, sales management, marketing and other self-help topics. He has also published fiction and non-fiction stories for children

As an illustrator and photographer, he has included his works in his own books and blogs. He enjoys hiking and mountain biking in the great outdoors and taking long walks in the woods with his dog.

Currently he is an active Realtor in Michigan and frequent community volunteer. He is a member of the National Association of Realtors, The Council of Residential Specialists, and the Michigan Association of Realtors. He is also an active member of the Battle Creek Area Association of Realtors where he was awarded 'Realtor of the Year' in 2010, and served as Board President in 2011. He founded his own independent publishing company in 2012.

To follow Michael:

www.MichaelDelaware.com

Facebook.com/MichaelDelawareAuthor

Goodreads.com/MichaelDelaware

Amazon.com/Author/MichaelDelaware

Linkedin.com/in/MichaelDelaware

@MichaelDelaware

Other titles by the author available as eBooks:

The Art of Sales Management: Lessons Learned on the Fly (also available in print)

The Art of Sales Management: Revelations of a Goal Maker (also available in print)

Small Business Marketing: An Insider's Collection of Secrets

Arts & Craft Shows: The Top 10 Mistakes Artist Vendors Make... And How to Avoid Them!

Arts & Craft Shows: 12 Secrets Every Artist Vendor Should Know

Inspiration: The Journey of a Lifetime

For Real Estate:

Understanding Land Contract Homes: In Pursuit of the American Dream

Land Contract Homes for Investors

Going Home... Renting to Home Ownership in 10 Easy Steps

In Children's Fiction:

Scary Elephant Meets the Closet Monster

In Children's Non-Fiction:

My Name is Blue: The Story of a Rescue Dog

More titles will be available in print in late 2013 and in 2014. For a current list of available print books visit:

www.ifandorbutpublishing.com

If you enjoyed this book, don't overlook reading the first book in this series:

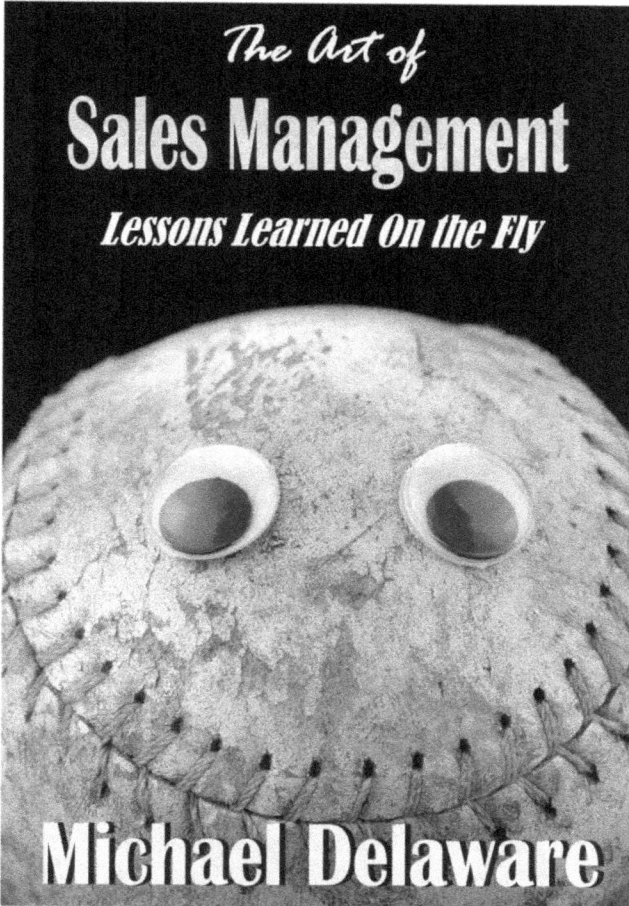

The Art of

Sales Management

Lessons Learned On the Fly

Michael Delaware

Available at major bookstores everywhere, and also through the publisher's website:

www.ifandorbutpublishing.com

Or the second book in this series:

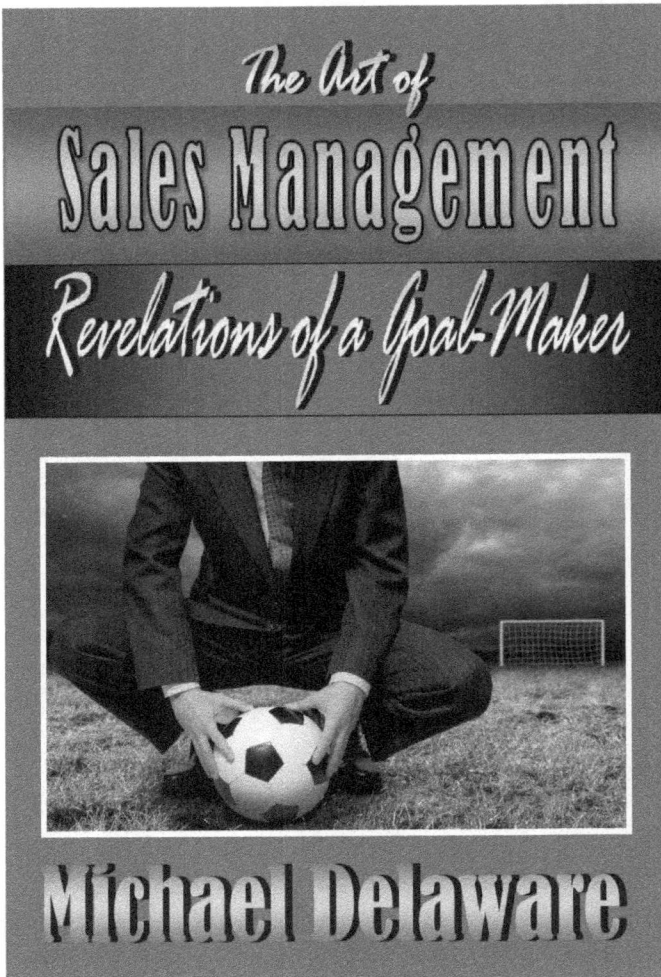

The Art of
Sales Management
Revelations of a Goal-Maker

Michael Delaware

Also available at major bookstores everywhere, and through the publisher's website:

www.ifandorbutpublishing.com

The Art of Sales Management

The Art of Sales Management series has a special website and blog that covers more information about forthcoming books, events and a new forum for discussion is coming soon in 2014.

You can find the website here:

www.artofsalesmanagement.com

www.ingramcontent.com/pod-product-compliance
Lightning Source LLC
Chambersburg PA
CBHW020200200326
41521CB00005BA/200